M000275893

THE ULTIMATE MARATHON

My Journey With Multiple Myeloma Cancer

Tim McNeill

DEDICATION

This book is dedicated to all of my family,
friends, and medical professionals that
have thought outside the box to help me
make it through the most challenging time
of my life.

It is especially dedicated to my sister Mary.

CONTENTS

ACKNOWLEDGMENTS

The book/journal you are about to read is being told by me, the
patient, who lived this experience, with input from my sisters,
who were aware of what was going on behind the scenes. It
tells where my family and I spent the better part of four years of
our lives. When you have a Mum and five sisters (Sue, Peg,
Julie, Mary and Trish) who are persistent and don't
accept the word "No", it makes for interesting reading.

When I was first diagnosed with multiple myeloma, a blood
borne cancer, my family started keeping daily journals
of everything that was going on in my presence and behind
the scenes. My family filled several journals, which included
medical information as well as their thoughts about what they
witnessed during this journey. In the end it wasn't just a
marathon, it was the ultra marathon; for myself, my family,
and my oncology doctor. He has never had a patient like me
 and probably never will.

I hope that readers are able to glean information from this book to
help them identify processes and lessons that may assist them with
their marathons.

Chapter One

The Diagnosis

Spring 2002. My back had been bothering me for quite awhile. I don't know exactly when it started but it gradually had gotten worse. It hurt right between my shoulder blades and the pain was nagging and constant so I resorted to taking Tylenol. Taking pain medication was not something I would normally do to resolve pain issues. I would work through pain by stretching, getting massages, soaking in ice baths or getting adjustments from my chiropractor. But this time none of those helped. After receiving multiple treatments from the chiropractor, he remarked that he couldn't help relieve the pain and said, "I've done as much as I could." I asked him for an x-ray of my spine and he said, "You had one three years ago and the picture would be the same."

I was getting frustrated. I needed to look for another solution for my back problem. The health club where I worked out at had a physical therapy business in the same building. I wanted to see what they had to say about my condition so I went in for a consult. I explained to the physical therapist how long I had been having this pain in my back, where it was, and what he thought could be a possible solution to the problem. His course of treatment was a routine of several exercises, which would strengthen my back muscles. It sounded like a good start. The pain was raising all the red flags in my mind. I didn't walk out of any of my physical therapy appointments with the same feeling of my back being sore like it had been when I saw other back specialists. The problem was it wasn't getting better. I had hit a wall in my rehab.

To compound the problem, my insurance was going to cover only so many appointments. We needed to do as many exercises that the physical therapist thought would help.   I was frustrated as it's not where I thought I'd be when my insurance coverage ran out. I had the exercises to do the rehab at home during the week, but was it going to help? The pain continued and started to increase in intensity. I was trying to figure out what my next move should be. Who can steer me in a better direction? I decided to talk to some people that had back problems and see what options they had taken to alleviate their pain.

My niece suggested seeing a doctor of kinesiology, which provides treatment through strength and conditioning, rehabilitation, and exercise. She had gotten good results with her back situation from this doctor. I remember in my initial meeting with the kinesiologist that he stated, "I think I've seen what you've had before so I can help you." But over the course of our appointments I wasn't seeing any progress and was getting more frustrated. I decided to go in another direction.

I went to see another chiropractor, who a co-worker said did an amazing job with helping his ailing back. My sister Julie went with me to see what this doctor had to say. He was the first one who mentioned that he wanted to take a full length picture of my entire back. Most x-ray machines can't take full length pictures of the entire spine but this doctor had a machine that could. I remember sitting down in a meeting room with Julie and the doctor to go over the x-rays. He had this concerned look on his face, and he warned me that what he was about to show me wasn't normal. The x-rays showed that the area between my shoulders where I was having the most pain was because the vertebrae had collapsed and was putting strain on other parts of my spine.

He indicated that he could help me with the pain. My sister questioned him again about helping with the pain, and he assured us he could. Based on what the x-rays showed and what he said he could do, I decided to give this a try. I was willing to try anything. The difference between his methods and the others I had tried was that he wanted me to go for a short walk right after my appointment. His thinking was that walking would take away the soreness from the back and neck adjustments he was performing. I'd take a walk right outside his building before I would leave after my appointment. He said it would take two to three weeks for me to feel a difference in my back.

It was during this time that my appetite started to change. I wasn't very hungry anymore. All I wanted to do was drink liquids. After about two and a half weeks of going to this doctor I wasn't getting any better. I couldn't sleep in my bed anymore; I had to sleep in the recliner to get any sleep. I was also losing weight and I rarely ever lost weight. My normal weight was between 185 and 190 pounds. Usually, I stayed pretty much at the same weight all of the time, so yeah, I was worried about what was going on. Some people who hadn't seen me on a regular basis noticed right away how different I looked. A soccer coach, who is a friend of my sister Mary and her husband Andy, noticed right away after not seeing me for eight months. Andy also noticed the difference when it was pointed out to him by the coach. This was right before I was diagnosed.

I scheduled an appointment with my primary doctor, Dr. Smith, to see if he could diagnose the problem. When I was finally able to see him, I explained my symptoms; loss of appetite, loss of weight, drinking lots of fluids, and my back pain was intensifying. I asked him if he was going to draw some blood and he said no. He concluded that I had the stomach flu and that it would pass and if it didn't, he wanted me to come back in two weeks. I left my appointment confused with his assessment.

I don't usually get sick, other than catching a head or chest cold twice a year. I've never had the stomach flu before, but these symptoms and his diagnosis didn't make sense to me. Did Dr. Smith hear what I was telling him about my symptoms, or was he running late for his next patient? I wasn't going to wait two weeks to see him again, so I scheduled another appointment for the following week. My symptoms were still the same. I had lost about twenty pounds during the last six months and weighed about 165 pounds. My pants were really baggy around my waist now, and I had to wear a belt to hold up my britches.

June 8, 2002. I remember sitting in the waiting area for my appointment, scratching my head, trying to figure out what was going on with my health. I had never felt like this before. I had never lost this much weight before. I had never had this much pain in my back before. What the hell was going on with my body? I was hoping to get some answers because I was worried that something was seriously wrong.

When the nurse called me into his office, I climbed onto the exam table and laid flat on my back to minimize the pain. Dr. Smith came in and asked how I felt. In detail, I explained how my condition hadn't changed for the better. I wasn't eating and my back was bothering me more. I told him I wanted my blood checked to see if that showed anything. My sister Peggy, who I lived with at the time, recommended that I get a blood test. The doctor had the nurse come in and draw some blood. I lay on the exam table waiting for some answers. It seemed like I was waiting forever for him to return, but now I know why.

He had a manila envelope in his right hand and a concerned look on his face. "Well, what did the tests show?" I asked curiously. "Did you find out what's wrong with me?" He looked at me and said, "Your blood work shows that you have cancer."

WOOOOOOOOAA! What did he just say? Did I hear him right? The air felt like it had just been sucked out of the room. I had a difficult time breathing, and it took a few moments to catch my breath. My mind started racing about what he had just said. Did I hear him right? Did he say I had cancer? How could that be? I am only 38 years old.

I have been an athlete my whole life and have taken care of my body. I ate right, exercised daily, didn't drink, didn't smoke, and had never used drugs. This didn't make any sense to me. He started telling me about what actions he had already taken in calling the hospital and telling them I was on my way. He gave me the manila envelope, which contained my medical history and his notes, and I left the office. It felt like my shoulders were touching the floor as I walked out in the waiting area. The weight of the world...well, that's what it felt like at the time. I couldn't believe it. I called my boss Andy, who is also my brother-in-law, to come and pick me up at the clinic because it was close to work and asked him to give me a ride uptown to the hospital. I was going to leave my car at the clinic and someone from work could stop by to drive it back to work. I didn't really care too much about it at that point. I remember Andy saying something to me as we were driving uptown to the hospital, but I wasn't listening. My mind was still racing. Andy knew something was up, so I told him what the doctor had said. I was in a fog the whole way to the hospital.

It seemed like it took forever to get there and as he dropped me off in the emergency drop-off area, I gave him the keys to my car, thanked him for the ride, and set out to find the admission desk. Just like that I went from going back to work to going into the hospital with the diagnosis of having cancer.

Once I walked through the hospital doors, the admission desk was just inside the entrance. I sat down and went through the whole nine yards of giving my personal and insurance information to an admission's representative. I didn't want to go through this. My mind was still hazy about what I had been told an hour ago. When we finished the admission process the representative directed me to the part of the hospital where I'd be admitted. I went to the third floor that was called the critical care unit for the as- yet diagnosed patients. I was directed to my room and changed into a hospital gown. The floor nurse came in and asked me some more questions about my symptoms and completed a blood draw. I told the nurse about how bad the back pain was, that I had already taken sixteen ibuprofen today, and it was not helping with the pain.

The nurse wanted to get as much background information as possible, so she could relay it to the doctor who would be assigned to my case. Dr. Smith, my primary doctor, showed up. I don't know why. There was nothing he could do for me now. I didn't need to see him at all because he told me I only had the stomach flu. He was probably concerned that he could have a malpractice lawsuit against him, since he sent me home at my first appointment, telling me I only had the flu.

Andy called my Mum about our trip to the hospital, and she contacted the rest of the family. I should mention here that I come from a big family, 5 sisters, 4 brothers, their spouses, and many nieces and nephews.

Notes from Peg – "Damn, my cell phone was ringing!" I said to myself as I was leaving my last home visit for the day; it was 2:47 pm. As a geriatric Social Worker and single mother of two daughters, I still had another 8 hours of things to take care of before I could go to bed. I looked at my cell phone display and saw it was Mum calling; I answered, "Hi Mum, what are you doing?" Mum said, "Tim is at the hospital Peg. Can you meet us there?" Mum sounded concerned and her voice was unusually quiet.

I stopped my running mid-step and dropped half of the work papers in my hands and asked, "What did you say? Did Timmer get hurt at work?" Mum quietly said, "Just meet us at the hospital."

My parents, sisters and their spouses started to show up at the hospital shortly after I was admitted. Peg parked her car and ran into the hospital. She knew her way through the hallways and where I was being seen, so she went flying into the waiting area and saw the rest of the family all around. She said everyone's eyes were piercing and their shoulders were all slumped. Two of my brothers, Scott and Tomas, arrived at the hospital a few hours later. They didn't know at the time what was going on. They just knew that tests were being done to diagnose my health issues. After finishing some tests, I was wheeled past family in the hall and back into my small emergency room. The nurse walking past Peg in the hall said, "He is very sick," and shook her head. Peg looked at her as she walked away from us down the hall and thought, "She must be confused."

Dad and some of my siblings came into the room. The rest of the family was nervously waiting in the family area with Mum. The waiting time seemed like hours.

The lab took forever to get the results back. The doctor wanted to be sure that the correct diagnosis was identified and what his action plan was going to be for the immediate future. My primary doctor had not even remotely revealed to me how serious this was. But now, it was going to be revealed to me and my family.

My family was told that the doctor would be coming in and the rest of them came to my room or stood right outside in the hall. When the oncology doctor arrived, I think he was surprised at the number of people waiting for him. He came into my room in his white doctor's coat, looking like he had some bad news to deliver. His name was Dr. Lowe.

He introduced himself to everybody and shook each person's hand. He was tall, a little over six feet, and didn't have a loud voice, but he had a confident delivery of his words. And he was very close to my age.

He shook my hand after he introduced himself and asked how I was feeling. I said I was feeling alright, and then he asked about my current symptoms as he examined me.

Peg gently grabbed for my Dad's hard-working right hand and squeezed it. She looked in his eyes and nodded her head, "This will be alright Dad." He had raised all ten of us kids to accept what we were "handed".

Dr. Lowe proceeded to explain that I had a blood borne cancer called Multiple Myeloma and was in stage 4A at that time. Peg gently dropped Dad's hand and covered her mouth…She knew what multiple myeloma was and the prognosis.

I had never heard of it before and did not know what stage 4 meant. Mum said that her sister had myeloma and my Grandma, on my Dad's side, died of leukemia, both blood borne cancers. Mum then asked how long Dr. Lowe thought I had it.

He explained that this type of cancer "smolders" in a person's body for 1 to 2 years before it surfaces in noticeable symptoms. He also explained what the stages were and how they were assigned. Stages 1A and 1B were the least severe stages. Stages 4A and 4B were the most critical and life threatening stages and were assigned based on how much the cancer had progressed.

Multiple Myeloma appears when uncontrolled multiplications of plasma cells occur. As these cells grow and take up more space in the bone marrow, bones weaken and cause pain, particularly in the ribs and back. Eventually, the growth of plasma cells interferes with the production of normal red blood cells, white blood cells and platelets. Unlike normal antibodies, which come in different molecular sizes and types, cancerous plasma cells (myeloma cells) produce antibodies of the same molecular type called monoclonal proteins or M proteins. Almost all cancers need a blood supply and initiate the formation of blood vessels through a process called angiogenesis. When their blood supply is interrupted, cancers stop growing and die. The medication I was going to be taking aims to decrease the blood supply to the cancer.

The doctor said that there wasn't a cure for it. The only thing I heard from what he had just said was the last part. I definitely heard that part...definitely. He also said I was anemic, dehydrated, possibly had pneumonia, had renal (kidney) failure and that I might need a kidney transplant. The bad news was all coming at once. He didn't mince words. I guess if I was going to hear bad news, I might as well hear it all at once. He talked about the treatment plan he was going to implement. He prioritized what my immediate needs were and ordered an IV to rehydrate me, as well as infuse some red blood for my anemia. He wanted to get my body built back up before starting any cancer treatments.

His next priority was to address my kidney problems. A urine test was taken and my creatinine level was 19.5, one of the highest levels the doctor had seen. The normal range for creatinine is .50 – 1.20 milligrams. The kidney function is measured by creatinine levels. The creatinine numbers are a big testing indicator for myeloma patients. Creatinine is produced from creatine, a molecule of major importance for energy production in muscles. Creatinine is transported throughout the bloodstream to the kidneys. The kidneys filter out most of the creatine and dispose of it in the urine. Creatinine levels that reach 10.0 or more, as in my case, indicate severe kidney impairment and the need to have dialysis to remove toxins from the blood.

Dr. Lowe indicated that I would need to immediately start dialysis 3 times a week to cleanse my blood and take the impurities out of my body. Once Dr. Lowe felt that the dehydration, anemia, possible pneumonia and kidney issues were more under control, he would begin the cancer treatments, which included chemotherapy drugs. I hate taking pills and had no clue what chemotherapy would do to my body, but I would do whatever it took to live. I think it's safe to say all my family was in shock at the seriousness of my illness and all the other health issues I had.

My Mum became overwrought with anger and disbelief after hearing the diagnosis and the treatment plan. Dr. Smith was sitting outside my room when all this was going on. When he saw my Mum coming up to talk to him, he put his head down.

Mum raised her voice and scolded him for not doing any blood tests or getting a urine sample from me at my first appointment with him. The thing about my Mum is she doesn't raise her voice very often, but when she does it feels like the most humiliating thing you have ever gone through. You feel about two inches tall when she talks down to you, and she is only 5 feet 2 inches tall. She's one of those people that can make you feel really bad about what you did to make her angry. Some of my family went out in the hall and some went back to the waiting area so the medical staff could have more space in my room.

Sue and Peg went down the hallway to talk, and Sue said I was in renal failure and that my kidneys were failing. Peg looked at her and screamed, "What??!! I didn't hear that. You have got to be kidding me! How much can one person take? What is going on?" She went to the closest hospital wall and started slapping it like she was spanking the building. This building was changing her entire perspective about life and living and fairness and the sanctity of our wonderful farm family.

The nurses came in and took my vitals right away and tried to place a needle in my right arm by my elbow. The problem was my veins were rolling, meaning there was not enough fluids in them for the needle to puncture and stay in, and so the nurse couldn't get the needle to where the IV would work. Again and again they tried to get the needle in, but it wasn't working. After eight times of poking my right arm with the needle the nurse moved over to my left arm. She didn't have any better luck with the left arm. I could tell the nurse was getting frustrated so she asked another nurse to give it a try. The second nurse wasn't having any luck either. After ten needle pokes in my left forearm, they called for a phlebotomist, who specializes in putting needles in patients to draw blood. The phlebotomist was even having trouble at first, but finally after a few times the IV went in my left forearm. My family started to enter the room after the medical staff left.

The only good news that I liked was that I was going to be able to go home the next day after being re-hydrated, and they monitored my condition overnight. I hate hospitals! I mean I really hate hospitals like the next person. The smell and everything about them makes me wary of them.

Once I was given my diagnosis and there was something concrete to go on, my family was told separately that the average survival rate for a person with Stage 4 myeloma was six months. Because of all the medical issues I had the family decided not to share this information with me at the time.

My sister's Sue, Mary, and brother Scott were in the room with me shortly after, and they prayed with me for complete healing. That was strange for all of us, since our family did not normally pray out loud together.

Dr. Lowe came back into my room and said he would be back in the morning to talk with me and the rest of the family and answer any questions we had.

The first night in the hospital was the worst, so many unknowns. My sister Julie came by my bedside and said to me, "Don't you dare give up. We're going to get through this." Yeah, I was real emotional at this point. Some of my family was in the waiting area deciding how to notify the rest of my siblings that were not there.

My sister Trish, who lived three hours away, had just given birth to my nephew Austin the day before. The family decided that Trish would be told a couple of days later, so she could enjoy the birth of her son. My sister Mary called Trish's husband a day later and told him about my diagnosis. A phone call was made to my brothers Steve and Mike, who lived in Portland, Oregon, to give them the bad news. They said they would make arrangements to fly home as soon as possible.

My family was leaving for the night and would be back the next day to learn as much as they could and decide what the next steps would be. That was one of the longest nights of my life. I didn't sleep much, my mind was racing. My thoughts now were "it's all about getting through the next day." One day I'm going in to see my doctor, the next day I'm getting treated for cancer. It didn't seem real to me yet that this was happening, but I had to deal with it like everybody else. The nurses came in multiple times throughout the night to check my vitals and change my IV medications. I didn't realize that this would be the routine whenever I was in the hospital over the next four years.

Notes from Peg - Peg had to figure out how to tell her two daughters Reeannon and Rachel that their Uncle Tim and their housemate was very ill. Their dad had died suddenly in an accident when they were 12 and 10, and then their paternal uncle died suddenly a year after their father's accident from an unexpected heart attack.

Peg had decided to move her family closer to our big farm family and asked me if I would like to live together and be a positive male role model for the girls. Of course I said yes and Peg was overjoyed. Eventually our brother Scott had moved in with us, and we began to create a whole new family together.

When Peg was driving home she thought she hadn't been a good sister and should have been more helpful to me when I said something about the pain in my back. She thought that I was having back issues like the rest of us had. We were all hard workers and back pain was just part of working hard.

When she got home she sat down with the girls in the living room and Reeannon asked, "Okay, so what's wrong with Uncle Tim?" Peg looked at the kitchen clock, for no particular reason, but she knew that she wanted to avert showing them her own well of tears that would surely and slowly be forthcoming. She choked out the words, "He's in the hospital with a rare form of cancer." And for the first time in their lives, they were quiet…

The next morning Dr. Lowe came to my room and by this time my family was already there. He shared that he wanted me to stay in the hospital a few more days to build my body back up and start some antibiotics after seeing some of the lab results. He hadn't seen a case like mine before to base his treatment protocol on. I thank God he contacted the National Myeloma Center in Little Rock, Arkansas. The doctors from the center reviewed my medical case from the records he sent them, and they provided him with recommendations on treatments. I give him a lot of credit for doing that. Doctors don't usually have consults with other doctors in other healthcare networks. He talked about my cancer treatment; the medications that he felt would give me the best chance of survival, and the side effects of the drugs.

Thalidomide and Dexamethazone would be the chemotherapy drugs he would prescribe. The drug combination that Dr. Lowe determined would be the best option for my myeloma was called BTD, short for the drug names Biaxim, Thalidomide and Dexamethazone (or "Dex for short). In order to use the Thalidomide there was a specific protocol to follow in order to purchase it. Thalidomide was administered in the 1950s and 1960s for anxiety and insomnia and for morning sickness for pregnant woman. Then pregnant woman began to have more infant deaths and babies with birth defects, such as missing arms or legs. It was taken off the market for 30 years until some researchers found that it was beneficial to use in conjunction with Dexamethazone, in the treatment of Multiple Myeloma.

I didn't realize it at the time, but I was being considered for a clinical trial in using Thalidomide. In a drug clinical trial, patients receive specific medications according to the research plan or protocol created by researchers of a drug company. When a product or approach is being studied, it is not usually known whether it will be helpful, harmful, or any different than available alternatives (including no intervention). The researchers try to determine the safety and effectiveness of the medication by measuring certain outcomes in the patients. Like most medications there could be side effects including low white blood cell count (which makes your body more susceptible to infection) and neuropathy (which damages a single nerve or nerve group and results in loss of movement, sensation, or other function of that nerve). Generally, neuropathy occurs in a person's arms, fingers or feet and can be permanent.

Each month Dr. Lowe would have to contact the drug company, enter certain information regarding my case, and indicate what drug and dosage would be purchased. The drug company gave Dr. Lowe an authorization number, which he would write on the prescription.

The prescription would be given to my sister Sue and she would call the drug company monthly, use the authorization number to access their system and complete a phone survey, which asked if I was using the drug correctly and only for the intended purpose.

In order to pick up the drug at the pharmacy she would contact the pharmacy to tell them that someone would be bringing in a prescription for the Thalidomide the following day. Pharmacies don't normally stock this medication, so they would have to order it. I later found out that some people were charged as much as $13,000 a month for this drug. I also found out how good my health insurance was because my co-pay for paying for the drug was a fraction of the cost.

I was concerned with the short term side effects since the list was long: having a sleepy or drowsy allergic reaction, red itchy rash, fever, fast heart beat and dizziness. I wasn't on board right away with taking the medications and dealing with the side effects. This was a lot of information to take in at one time. How the heck was my body going to be able to handle all of these side effects? Do I have any other options or was this it? Was this the most immediate action we could take? Did I need to make a decision like right now? Yeah, that about covers it for all the major questions I had at the time. All the information was coming so quick then, but because of the seriousness of my illness Dr. Lowe felt he could not afford to wait much longer to begin my treatment.

I never heard of Thalidomide before. Then again, I didn't know any well known cancer medications to begin with. My knowledge of drugs included aspirin, antibiotics or pain killers, which I used whenever I was injured while playing football. Other options at this point weren't immediate enough for my doctor's liking. So many things were being told to me at once, and I was happy when I was told that someone in the family was writing down all this information; I could read it later and absorb it more. Even though I was nervous about it, I started taking the medication, as well as some other pills. Then they told me they would be moving me to a room on the sixth floor, the oncology floor.

I didn't know this until later but shortly after my diagnosis, based on their statistical research, my sister Mary and her husband Andy sat down with their three daughters and told them the chances were that I would pass away fairly soon. That was a shock to hear.

After I was moved to my room, the hospital social worker came in and talked about me designating someone to be my health care power of attorney and financial power of attorney. My sister Peggy is a social worker, so I chose her as my health care power of attorney and my sister Sue, who works in the field of finance, volunteered as my financial power of attorney. Now that the legal stuff was out of the way I could concentrate on my survival.

I'm sure my co-workers knew something was up. Yah think? I don't know if my boss told them what he knew, and I really didn't care what he told them. I know this, news travels fast, but bad news travels faster.

Keeping everyone informed on a daily basis was important to the entire family. Every morning a family member would be in my room before the doctor came in during morning rounds. When he came in they'd take detailed notes on what was said and discussed what the plan was for the day and what tests had been scheduled. They'd always, always ask questions on my behalf. If they didn't understand the answer, they would ask the doctor to provide an answer in plain English, not in medical terms. Keeping everyone in the family informed was tough, but I had family who took the effort to make it work. They used the telephone tree every day. One person would call the next and pass on any information received from the medical staff that morning, and emails were sent out so those that lived further away would also be kept up to date.

When all my family members were in town at the same time, it made sense to have them tested to see if anyone would be a possible match for a bone marrow transplant. We were getting a little ahead of ourselves, but we wanted to be prepared for every option. We wouldn't find out the results for awhile but you have to think, with nine brothers and sisters, that I'd match at least one of them. About a month after the testing was completed, the transplant coordinator contacted my sister Sue and said they had identified that I had a broken chain in my DNA. They were wondering if our parents would come in and get tested as well to determine if one of them also had a broken chain. This was purely for research purposes. Because my health issues were so serious, Sue decided to not even ask the parents to participate in the testing. They already had a lot on their minds.

Since I was cooped up in my hospital room, I tried to keep my body limber by stretching my legs on the bed. I normally exercised every day at home. When Dr. Lowe was informed of what I was doing, he told me that I could not do that anymore because it could cause more damage to the bones in my body. I could see his point, but for me it helped with the tension in my body.

While I was in the hospital my family decided to get my living situation set up in a more beneficial way. I was in the process of selling the house I lived in with my sister Peg and brother Scott. I decided, well I think my parents decided, that I should stay at their house now since we were selling ours. It made sense since they were both retired, and they could help with my daily care. What a godsend those two were. My parents lived in a two story farm house that was built in the early 1900s. They decided that I should stay in a bedroom on the first floor, so it was easier for me to get around, and I wouldn't have to go up and down the stairs to the second floor. My brothers and sisters wallpapered and painted the bedroom I was going to be sleeping in. It looked like something you'd see transformed on the cable channel TLC, where they makeover a room. They did a great job in a short amount of time!

In order for me to be able to go home from the hospital, I would need to receive daily infusions of antibiotics for my pneumonia and those infusions would be given by a family member.

A schedule was set up with a home health nurse to train my sisters and Dad on how to give them. The one thing about having my family give me infusions was that they would have to stick a needle in my vein and well, I wasn't too confident in them getting the hang of it. The home health nurse showed them how to best get the desired results and what to look for when they're doing the procedure. The IV's had a clear line that ran from a clear bag to a needle, so you could see it dripping all the way down the line. That's how you knew when it was working, when the IV was consistently dripping. They all got the hang of it very quickly.

My sisters were more worried about sticking me with a needle than my Dad was. He didn't have any problem.

My Dad was surprisingly the best out of all of them in giving me my infusions, and he was 73 years old. When my sisters had a question about if the infusion was working correctly, they would ask him. He never had a bad day with giving me infusions. Even when something went wrong he could tell by the way the drip was going and he'd start over. I think he would have been a great home health nurse if he wanted, you know "old school military style". He became very proficient at it. He also gave me my daily neupogen shots with a small needle in my belly. This was given to help boost my immune system. Dad didn't have any problems doing that either. He was a natural.

Between my dialysis appointments three times a week, for three hours each time, and seeing my oncology doctor following tests, my parents and two or three of my sisters were driving back and forth a lot to the clinics, which were approximately 30 miles away. It would take a half a day just to go to one appointment.

The dialysis nurse recommended that the hospital put in a PICC line (Peripherally Inserted Central Catheter) in my upper arm. The line snakes through the upper body to stop near a large vein, which can feed intravenous fluid near the heart area. The idea for me to get a PICC line was to minimize the number of times that I would get stuck with a needle. The PICC line lessens the chances of getting an infection from the needle because there already is an entry point for the line in my arm. It's like having a fire hydrant where you can connect a hose to it. PICC lines can be left in a patient for up to two months.

According to a medical clinic health book, as a rule, most people on dialysis require 8 to 12 hours of dialysis a week. Acute renal failure, which is what I was diagnosed with, can be reversible and some people recover in one to two months. It could take up to a year to regain full function of the kidneys.

Complications can come in the form of infections from the process itself. The dialysis machine is designed to artificially cleanse the blood of waste products since the kidneys are no longer able to do so. One of the signs of renal failure is a yellowish brown cast to the skin, which my Mum had remarked about upon learning of the renal failure. Who would have guessed that was one of the issues I was dealing with, certainly not any of my doctors at that time.

The dialysis was going as smoothly as it could. My Dad would usually be the one to take me to my appointments. The dialysis center required someone to drive you home after your appointment. I didn't have a problem with my Dad driving me, except for his reaction when we didn't beat the stop lights. The main street up to the dialysis center has a lot of traffic lights and if you don't catch the lights just right, you would be stopping every two hundred yards for a red light. My Dad tried to time the lights so he made it through them without stopping, and when he didn't he got pissed off and started yelling things I can't print. It's funny at first hearing him get mad, but by the end of the trip I was thinking he was going to get out and beat up those traffic lights. When we got to the dialysis center I'd take a long deep breath. I'll say this, my Dad is anything but boring to live with.

My Mum devised a daily medication system which told me what to take and when. It was a spreadsheet of information written down on paper regarding days, times of day and amounts of medications. I don't think she knew what she made out was a spreadsheet of every consumable pill and directions. Depending on the day of the week, I could be taking 8-10 different medications. My Mum has very neat, very readable penmanship and it's easy to recognize her handwriting.

Everything was going fine that first week. It didn't take long for me to lose my taste of food taking that many pills a day. One of the chemotherapy drugs I was on, Dexamethazone, tends to cause a person to lose their taste for food. I lost my appetite, so consequently I had to force myself to eat, even though I couldn't taste it. My Mum was heckling me to eat, eat, eat! She wanted me to gain some of the 30 pounds back that I had lost before being diagnosed. When you can't taste the food you're eating, it's like eating plain oatmeal all day without adding any sugar.

Mum made an appointment to meet with the hospital dietician to find out what foods worked well with the medications I was taking.

She bought a cookbook called, "Cooking for Cancer". There were suggestions on what foods to eat before starting chemotherapy to help minimize the nausea during chemotherapy, and when chemotherapy was done. There were suggestions on foods to eat when constipated due to the medications, when you have a sore throat after being on the ventilator, and what to eat to help increase your iron levels and energy. It helped Mum to be focused on one aspect of my care, since she is such a good cook and knows what I like or don't like. Otherwise, all of this would be overwhelming for her.

I would get somewhat tired from the dialysis but that was to be expected. The room I would normally have the dialysis performed in had a clock like the ones you see in the grade schools. I remember it because the room was pretty small, and the clock was about five feet above me on the wall. I'd be sitting in a recliner while the procedure was going on, but it was hard to take a nap during this time.

The first few times I went to dialysis I was amazed at the number of people that would come in for their procedures. You have to do whatever it takes to survive, and the majority of those people that would come in for their dialysis had kidney issues that could potentially kill them. I normally would get the same nurse every time that would hook up the dialysis machine and monitor me. She was easy to get along with, and I felt a little relieved when she was doing my procedure. I didn't really have too much time to think about what all was going on. The newness and shock of what had transpired over the last week wore off in a hurry and the routine of going to appointments and taking daily medications took over.

Chapter Two

My Condition Changed for the Worse—Quickly

The start of the second week was going well. My lab numbers were starting to improve. My Mum and sister Peg were going to go with me to my dialysis appointment on this day, giving my Dad a break from driving uptown. My doctor even remarked that I was getting better at the time. I've learned that things can change in a hurry though.

My dialysis appointment was going well and then, just like that, I started to get a change in my vital signs. I was getting the chills and I developed a fever. My sister Peg could tell by looking at me that I wasn't right, so we went directly to the hospital which, thank God, was only a few minutes away from the dialysis center. The checking in process never goes quick when you're trying to get into the hospital. It seems to go even slower when you're sick like I was, and you just want to get into a hospital bed. There's not always a bed available so the hospital has to move beds around to accommodate a new patient. Maybe that's what happened in my case because it seemed like it was taking forever. I was sitting in a wheelchair because of my back pain. I know I'm whining, but an hour seems like forever when you have a temperature and my back was getting really sore. I needed to lie down.

I had a temperature of 101.5, which is the minimum temperature you have to have to be admitted. I was finally checked in and taken to my room on the seventh floor. The nurses hooked me up to a monitor right away and put a monitor on my left finger to check my pulse ox regularly. The pulse ox tells you how much oxygen is getting to your fingers or toes. It should generally be between 93% and 100%. The first order of business was to try and get my temperature down and figure out what the problem was.

The next thing was to get a chest x-ray to see what my lungs looked like. I just had an x-ray of my lungs a week before but that can change in a hurry, so a new x-ray would be best to see what is currently going on. I was coughing up small amounts of blood with my sputum, which could indicate a number of things were happening. The x-ray would only show so much. Dr. Lowe was being very thorough. He requested that my brothers come home from Portland, Oregon because my condition had become more serious. My lungs were congested, and I couldn't cough anything up. He was concerned that I would not be able to survive having pneumonia. The myeloma was making my bones brittle from my deteriorating condition. I did not realize at the time the amount of damage that had been done to my skeletal system. I know it sounds scary, but it changed just that fast.

My nurse, who had given me the dialysis treatments, came to see me a couple of times. I always felt that it was odd that she was feeling so bad about me getting an infection. I could sense from her sad expression when she visited me that something happened with my dialysis treatments that I didn't know about at the time. It was a couple of years later, when I had the time to look at the doctors notes, that I found out that I had contracted a staph infection from an infected dialysis tube. I also had complications related to the cancer. I had been on dialysis for only two weeks so far.

My sister Julie remembers a conversation she had outside my room with Dr Lowe. It was only days after I was admitted that my condition started to deteriorate. My condition looked grave, and he brought up the idea of moving me to a hospice facility. He said he didn't know what else to do. That caught Julie off guard. She wasn't expecting him to say that. My whole family was scared when Julie told them what the doctor said.

My siblings called their kids to tell them of my situation and they all came to the hospital over the course of the next few days. I was not aware that Dr. Lowe had brought up the hospice option and felt that since I was getting all these visitors that my condition had gotten a lot worse.

Notes from Peg - Tim's voice was raspy today. She could barely understand what I was saying. Tim was feverish and clearly in pain. The doctor was just leaving the room when Peg got there, and Tim started yelling at him, "Doc, come back! What are you trying to tell me?" Peg looked for the doctor and asked him to come back to Tim's room. He said that Tim had a staph infection that had probably started at the site of the dialysis port. There were bacteria being carried in his blood throughout his entire body. The doctor then had to leave the room. It was then we knew that we were lucky enough to have this special doctor, who cared deeply for Tim as a patient, and whose compassion throughout this process would be considered nothing short of *INCREDIBLE*...

My pulmonologist was so concerned about the staph infection that he called a meeting with my family to discuss what was going on and what the next steps would be. My condition is very critical, he said, how critical only time would tell. My family, namely my Mum, was questioning why the doctor who treated my pneumonia during my first hospital stay sent me home with pneumonia. She asked point-blank if they'd discharged me for insurance purposes. The pulmonologist replied angrily, "I've been a pulmonologist for thirteen years, and I have never discharged anybody for insurance reasons." But the truth was Dr. Lowe took the recommendation of the pulmonologist; it was his decision that I be released. From this action, came the current dire period of events. Emotions were high. It must have been hard for Mum and Dad to see one of their children in such pain and not be able to fix it for me.

Chapter Three

All I Remember Is Waking Up in the ICU

July 2, 2002. The day started off like any other Sunday morning for me in the hospital. My sister Sue always stopped by with the morning newspaper, and today she asked me if I wanted her to stay, and I said, "Yes". I had a very deep cough but wasn't coughing anything up, so it was hard on my lungs. I had either torn cartilage or broken a rib on my right side, but I didn't know which one. It hurt to cough, and the harder I coughed the worse it hurt.

As Sue was walking out into the hall and Mary and Scott were about to enter my room, I started to thrash around in my bed because I couldn't catch my breath. Sue saw what was happening and called the nurse. The nurse paged the doctor and two oncology doctors rushed in. One of the doctors was Dr. Lowe who was "on the floor" doing his regular rounds. He was on call that weekend, so I was lucky that he was there in the hospital at the time.

The doctors came out of my room after a few seconds and explained to Sue that I had a mucous plug in my throat that was blocking my airway and I couldn't catch my breath. Dr. Lowe asked Sue if she would give them permission to put me on a ventilator to help me breathe. Dr. Lowe's colleague was also in the room and explained to Sue that 50 percent of the people that they put on the ventilator don't ever come back off it and breathe on their own. Sue said she felt that Dr. Lowe's colleague was trying to talk her out of giving her permission. This was only the first of many times that Sue felt this colleague implied that it was a waste of time and expense in doing anything extra to prolong my life, because of the stage I was at. She eventually gave him the nickname,
"Dr. Doom and Gloom".

I don't know how long it took her to make her decision, but she said "yes" and they pulled the curtain around my bed to give them some privacy while they inserted the tube into my lungs. A couple of nurses were in the room, and one of them gave me a sedative to calm me down. In about twenty minutes they had put the ventilator in. A ventilator is a machine which doctors use for patients who cannot breathe in enough air on their own. A tube is put down the throat into the lungs, and the tube is connected to a machine that pushes and pulls air in and out of the lungs. In other words, you're breathing with the assistance of a machine now instead of on your own. How long I would be on it nobody knew. That was the scary part. In talking with Sue later she said it was a no brainer in giving permission to put me on the ventilator. She thought that my throat was clogged with the mucous plug, like a drain and the ventilator would unclog my plumbing.

The doctors asked my family to go to the waiting room around the corner from my room while the nurses transferred me to the intermediate intensive care unit (IICU). Once a patient is put on the ventilator they are automatically moved to IICU to be monitored more closely. Mary called my Mum and Dad, who were at the airport dropping off my brother Mike, who was heading back to Portland, Oregon and they all came back to the hospital.

Notes from Peg - We had gone to a parade on that Sunday in a town not far from where we lived. Yes, I felt guilty about not being at the hospital but the girls, my fiancé Dan, and I had scheduled this fun event with friends weeks before. My cell phone rang during the parade. I saw that sister Sue was calling. I looked at Dan and said, "It must be about Tim." We stopped breathing for a few moments as we heard a new phrase I had never heard before - something called a "mucous plug." We were to come to the hospital immediately...

The IICU had a whole new set of rules that visitors had to follow when they entered the room. You could only have one person in the room at a time. When I was taken to the IICU, my family was told what to expect about the machines, the tubes, and the hospital masks and gowns they'd have to wear every time they came into the room. I was sedated when they put me on the ventilator. I don't remember any of it until I woke up in the IICU. I tried to move my hands to feel what was in my mouth, and I couldn't. I looked over to my left to see why I couldn't reach up with my hand, and saw a restraint around my wrist. A nurse explained to me what was going on. Earlier, while sedated, I had pulled out the ventilator tube and that's why they had put me in restraints.

It took me a little bit of time to figure out where I was and what was going on. I had been asleep all day, and by now it's around four o'clock in the afternoon when I woke up. Dr. Lowe came in the room after the nurse had told him I had come out of the sedation. He first told me why I was on the ventilator to calm my fears, and then how long I would be on it. They were going to try to "wean me off of it" and would feed me through my nose tube because there was tape over most of my mouth to hold the ventilator tube in.

My sister Peg told the nurse there were twelve people in my family. The nursing staff figured the best thing to do was to put a small table outside my door with all of the clothing that people would have to wear to enter the room. You had to wear blue cloth hospital gowns along with a face mask and rubber gloves to help keep my room sterile.

When I first saw my family members wearing the required hospital attire, it looked weird, especially when I saw my Mum and Dad. But, like everything else in life, you see it long enough and you get used to it.

You could only wear the hospital gown once when you entered the room, and then you had to put it in the laundry bin to be washed. My family went through so many gowns that the nursing staff changed them over to wearing the disposable gowns. The problem with disposable gowns was that they kept the person's body heat confined, and it was like wearing a sweat suit for losing weight. I know how it felt too because I'd be wearing those gowns down the road. When I first woke up and realized where I was, the nurse asked me if I was going to yank out my tube and I shook my head no. But that's what patients usually say to begin with. The nurse didn't take the restraints off right away but she loosened them up. Eventually, once I became more aware of where I was and the nurse decided I wasn't going to go wild with my tube; she untied one strap on one side to see how I'd react. Once I was coherent and able to answer "yes" or "no" to most questions, and I could handle the surroundings, the nurse untied the other strap.

The bed they put me on in the IICU was a special bed that would slightly roll from one side to the other. It was supposed to help my back be more comfortable as well as avoid getting bed sores. It took a little time to get use to a rolling bed, but after awhile, if the bed wasn't moving I couldn't relax and rest.

The nursing staff was very strict that only one visitor could be in my room at a time. Initially, I was able to nod or shake my head no when they asked questions. Eventually they brought in a notepad for me to write on. I couldn't write with my right hand because they had so many IV's in my right wrist that it was too restricted and weak to use. I had to learn how to print using my left hand and to this day, I can barely make out what I was trying to write on that notepad.

The temperature outside was 100 degrees and my room was 80 degrees. I don't know if the air conditioning wasn't working, but I needed a large upright fan to cool my body off.

One fan wasn't enough so my family went and found another one. I had two fans going all the time. We kept the drapes closed all the time to keep out the heat from the sun. That was depressing for me not to be able to see outside. I'd have my brother, sister or nurse put a cold wash cloth on my head almost nonstop. There was a white styrofoam bucket they'd put ice in with water and dip the wash cloth in to cool my head. I don't know if it was my condition or what, but it was a struggle every day to keep my temperature down. My brother Tomas was a godsend in keeping me cool. He waited on me hand and foot during this time. He took time off from his job to see that I was taken care of in the ICU.

When I was I writing on the notepad, I'd ask a lot of short questions and requests. Is it raining outside? Can you move the fan so it blows on my feet? Can you put a wet towel on my head? Check on me occasionally. Can you find me a fluffy pillow for my neck? It's a lot cooler today in the room than yesterday. Since it was so hot in my room, all of my writing concerned staying cool. The doctors left just enough of an opening around the ventilator tube in the right corner of my mouth, so a green foam lollipop swab soaked in water could be put in my mouth when I was thirsty. I went through many of those green swabs to moisten my lips, and it felt good to swallow the water in the swab.

Someone in my family was staying over every night in the lounge area and checking up on me throughout the night to see if I was alright and needed to change the wash cloth on my forehead. The second or third night I was in IICU my sister Mary stopped in around 9:00 pm, shortly after Julie left. I told Mary I was tired of being in this hospital, and she nodded and said, "Yeah, we have to get you out of this place." I liked to hear Mary talk about her family, because it took my mind off being in the hospital even for a brief period of time. Mary told me her daughter Tasha got her butt kicked in soccer that day, but she's going to start over tomorrow!
I had to snicker.

Tonight, I had a slight temperature of 100.9 degrees. It seemed to go up more at night than during the day. I hated having a temperature because my head felt so hot. Mary stayed with me that night. After a day like this I needed a break, so Mary wanted to rent a movie. We needed to rent the video machine from the hospital, which stunk, but what are you going to do? I had a choice between "The Fast and the Furious" and "Meet the Parents." I had already seen both of them, but Mary hadn't seen "Meet the Parents," so I told her I hadn't seen it yet and that she could watch it for the first time.

As we started to watch the movie, one of my respiratory doctors walked in. He had a difficult question to ask. If they took me off the ventilator and I had another mucous plug, what would I want the doctors to do? I really didn't have much choice. I wanted to stay alive, so I told them that they should put me back on the ventilator. The one other option would be to do a tracheotomy, thus I didn't have to go back on the vent. That way I could be suctioned without being on the vent. This would be the last consideration in the event I wasn't able to clear the mucous. The only concern the respiratory doctor had about taking me off the ventilator was the secretions from my lungs. He said he was considering adding an order for steroids in a small dose which might help in reducing them. Before he left, he said he'd stop in the next day. Okay, finally we could hit "Play" and get back to the movie.

Dr. Lowe prescribed a drug, Zomata, to strengthen my bones. It takes three hours to administer, and as a result, the nurses would be checking on me all night. My brother Scott was staying overnight and checked on me at 11:25 pm. I haven't seen him much recently at the hospital, so when he's there we catch up on where my condition is at right now, and he tells me about his latest concrete job he's working on.

At 3:10 am, I woke up when they took my vitals and I fell back asleep at 3:20 am. The night nurse gave me some additional sleep medication. My vitals were checked again at 5:40 am and 6:10 am.

I had learned not to expect a solid night of sleep in the hospital because the nurses would come in throughout the night to take my vitals, no matter which hospital stay it was. I am worried about the long term effects of having the tube stuck down my throat. Since I couldn't get up and walk around I lost what little muscle I had. And being fed through a tube, I wasn't gaining any weight. I wonder if there's any damage to my esophagus.

I'd been thinking about the day when the vent is supposed to come out. The problem with coming off that machine is that it's not pleasant. I'll be coughing or spitting up, which is the best way to handle it. I'm already nervous because I don't know how my lungs will react. In the back of my mind I've been worrying about what Dr. Lowe's colleague said, "Fifty percent of the patients who go on the vent don't come back off of it". So that could be me. Yeah, I was concerned about the worst happening. Those thoughts crossed my mind.

Visiting hours ended at 8:00 pm and most people followed the rules and left the hospital by that time. But my family would always push the deadline, or stay later. From the time I was admitted until I was released three months later, somebody from my family stayed in the waiting room every night, though I didn't learn about that until months later. They had pillows and blankets all over the waiting room area. If they couldn't stay with me in the recliner or on a temporary bed in my room, they'd sleep in the waiting room.

I'm reading my sister Peggy's notes. On this particular day she was looking forward to coming to the hospital to see me. That must have been a crazy day for her as a social worker, to want to come to the hospital and see me in a bed on a ventilator!

The doctors came in today and touched certain points on my feet and ankles with their hands to see where I have feeling. The nurses asked me if I was tired when I was on the C-PAP (Continuous Positive Air Pressure). It's restrictive on my face and it makes me paranoid with also being on the vent.

The c-pap air flow is constant, meaning once the mask is tight on my face there is always air from the oxygen line blowing in my face. I was going to be wearing a Bi-Pap (Bi-level Positive Air Pressure) on all night. The bi-pap provides a stronger pressure during inhalation and light pressure during exhalation.

It's Saturday now, six days since I was put on the ventilator. The pulmonologist determined about a week after being on the ventilator that they would start to "wean me off the machine". They started by turning the machine off for two to five minutes to see how I would handle breathing on my own. Over the course of the next week they increased the amount of time they would shut the machine off. The machine made a lot of noise so it was nice and quiet when it was shut off. It took about one week to wean me off the machine. During that time it was very frustrating to continue to communicate with pencil and paper. The day they came in to tell me that they were ready to take the ventilator tube out, I was certainly ready. I knew it would be painful at the same time.

My sister Peggy is in tonight. She puts lotion on my elbows and my heels because my room is very dry and she puts some Vaseline on my chapped lips. That helps. I'm able to write with my right hand now. I laugh trying to read what I had written down with my left hand and seeing what I was trying to say. Most of it doesn't make sense, just random questions out of the blue. The medications I was on affected the way I was thinking.

One thing everybody picked up on when I wrote on the notepad was my need to be pulled higher up in the bed. My family could tell how I was positioned when I wasn't lying in the right spot at the head of the bed. I'd always end up sliding down to the foot of the bed. I couldn't pull myself back up because I was so weak and my back pain was excruciating. The nurses or my family would grab me under my arms and gently lift and pull me back up to the head of the bed. My brothers Steve and Mike were never easy on me when they pulled me back up the bed.

The next day my sister Sue had a strange experience with a nurse on the IICU floor. As she walked out into the hall the nurse asked her, "Are you a Christian?" and Sue replied, "Yes." The nurse went on to say, "You and your family are going on a long journey with your brother."

Sue didn't realize it at the time what the journey was she was talking about, but she realizes it now. Some journeys take you to places you have never been before and experience things you have never experienced before, and our entire family was on that type of journey. That was the second time my sister had someone ask if she was a Christian. She has always believed that the power of prayer is what has brought me and my family through this ordeal and that the prayers that were prayed during my first night in the hospital when I was diagnosed were being answered. She also believes that certain people are in your lives at certain times to help you get through stressful situations.

She has always felt that our sister Peggy was one of those people. She is a social worker for the elderly, but she also has many years of experience in dealing with catastrophic illnesses and knows how to assist families through the healthcare system and knows what resources are available to "soften the blow". Sue asked people from her church to come to the hospital and pray for me in the waiting room. I also found out that my Mum was going to mass every morning to pray for me. You never know everything that is going on behind the scenes for your benefit when you are ill.

Even before I was off the vent, my family had a million questions about different scenarios. For instance, will a steroid be given whenever the doctors hear a gurgling sound in my lungs upon examination? Will anything be changed regarding my meds or antibiotics? Do we have the right antibiotics pinpointed for the pneumonia? After I'm off the vent, how long will I stay in the intermediate ICU? Everybody was tense and wondered if my lungs would be able to handle not being on the ventilator, but nobody knew at this point. Those girls were always looking ahead and questioning all the choices my doctors were making. I was glad they were thinking aloud on my behalf. I needed all the help I could get.

I was told that my college football coach came to visit me while I was in the IICU. I also had other visitors come, but I wasn't in the mood for visitors, so the staff would ask them to write a short note for me and they would deliver it. It got crazy in my room the night before they were going to take the vent out. More tests were being run, antibiotics were being changed, and my vitals were continuously being checked. It was like Grand Central Station in my room. I hope I can relax enough to get a good night's sleep. Yeah, I'm nervous, but I'm glad the day is finally here.

July 13, 2002. It's day eleven, and for sure I'm coming off the ventilator today! I'm excited but also apprehensive about my breathing after having been on the machine for so long. Once I'm off the ventilator, the first 24-48 hours are going to be the toughest. I haven't used my lungs in almost two weeks, so I'll need to redevelop my lung strength. My secretions will be high early on, so I'll need to work on getting rid of the phlegm by spitting it out. I don't have a problem doing that! The problem is that I need to expand my lungs as much as possible without coughing. As my lungs expand and open up more, the secretions will go down.

When the nurse came in to take out the tube, she explained what she was going to do and what I needed to do. When she was ready, I was going to take a deep breath and blow it out while she pulled out the tube, continuing to breathe out until the tube was all the way out. When she actually started to pull the tube out, I couldn't believe how long it was, and I was running out of breathe by the time she finally had it all the way out. I was nervous, because I didn't know how I'd react breathing without the tube, so, I took a small breath, then a deeper breath, then I relaxed and I was breathing on my own! Finally, finally, finally, the vent tube was out. I guess I proved Dr. Doom and Gloom wrong and am part of the 50% that came off the vent successfully.

After that I was just trying to process everything in my mind, while the respiratory therapist came in frequently to check on how I was doing. It felt great to be able to drink from a glass. Since my throat was sore I whispered when talking to people for the first couple of days. They brought me food like chocolate pudding and applesauce as the first foods I could eat. It took a little while to get used to eating again. I'm going to be on the c-pap for two hours and off two hours initially. It feels good to be able to have my lips together. I'll still be writing on a notepad and moving my head to answer yes and no to questions and avoid talking as much as possible. The nurses finally took the ventilator machine out of my room. Good riddance! It was the first time I was able to see the machine that had kept me breathing for almost two weeks. I waved goodbye to it as they rolled it out of the room, like I was saying so long to an evil person. Hopefully, I'll never see that thing again. It felt like a huge weight had been lifted off my shoulders. What a relief!

Dr. Lowe is going to consult with the nutritionist about when the feeding tube will be coming out next. I'm currently taking in around thirty four hundred calories a day. The tube may come out in a couple of days. Chris, my nurse came in this evening and reminded us that the head of my bed needs to be at a 30 degree angle for two reasons. One is for the feeding tube and the second is the pneumonia.

It was great being off the ventilator, like being released from my restraints. I was looking forward to eating some real food that had some taste to it. And I was glad that I could sit up now and at least get wheeled outside for some fresh air if the weather was nice. Maybe I was being too anxious in my own personal predictions, but I was anxious to stand up and start walking again. The same day the tube was taken out I sat up in the recliner in my room. The doctor and nurses wanted me to sit in the chair most of the day if I could, but my back was really sore at this point. I needed to put a pillow behind my back to handle it. I lost a lot of weight too; down to around 130 lbs, so I was very weak. Once you are taken off the ventilator they move you out of the ICU and into a regular hospital room. I was moved to the 6th floor.

Notes from Peg - We would stay with our brother 24 hours a day during these dramatic medical episodes. We prayed, we worked our jobs, and then we would come to the hospital. This was our life during this time because this brother was OUR life. We watched him change before our eyes and his weight drop to only 126 pounds, but his soul and spirit still filled the room. We dug deep, we found our voices, and we learned many new important lessons about being *family*...

Chapter Four

The Clam Shell

By now I had multiple spinal fractures, and it seemed as if I was getting x-rays of my back almost every other day. The doctor didn't want to take a chance of damaging my back further because a couple of my vertebrae had already collapsed. The x-ray technicians decided that they would take my spinal x-rays while I was lying in bed. They would have to roll me to one side and place a hard x-ray board under me to take their pictures. It caused me a lot of pain. Now anytime I moved I experienced a lot of pain.

The skeletal x-rays showed I had collapsed vertebrae and my sternum was cracked. I could not take deep breaths because my lungs were being constrained by my cracked sternum. If your lungs cannot expand to full capacity it is easier to contract respiratory infections, because there is not enough oxygen to move the germs around in the lungs or to be able to take deep coughs. The infection settles in the bottom of the lungs and you can hear a crackling sound when you are breathing. My latest x-ray showed that there was more pneumonia (infection) on the left side of my lungs than on the right. The respiratory therapist would come in three times a day to work with me on trying to move the infection that was lying in the bottom of my lungs, by using a vibrating machine on my chest and back.

My back pain had become so severe and the vertebrae had become so weak due to the myeloma that a doctor, who specializes in designing body braces, was called in for a consult. He recommended the type of brace I'd need to wear to minimize further spinal damage. I'd seen back braces that people had worn out in public before, but the one I was going to be wearing would be custom made for me.

There was so much damage to my spine. The doctors felt I needed extra support. The physician explained the process of how the brace or clam shell would be made. A plaster cast would be made of the trunk of my body, both front and back. The cast was made like a typical cast for a broken bone you'd have on an arm or leg. I had to be lying down flat in the hospital bed while the brace technician formed the cast to my body. I had not laid flat on my back for more than two years due to the pain. The entire process would take around two hours, an hour for the front of my torso and an hour for my back. I had a bad feeling that this procedure was going to be total pain.

My brother Tomas was in the room the whole time asking if I needed anything, but all I needed was for the procedure to be done. I could not move while it was being formed, and it was hot and itchy throughout the whole process. They did the front of my torso first because they felt it would be less painful. It took an hour and went without a hitch, but I was still worried about my back. I imagined the technician would have to roll me to my side and place the plaster on a board on my bed which I would lay back on to mold the cast. The myeloma had really weakened my bones, and I was afraid this was going to do more damage. After all, I already had multiple compression fractures, and my sternum had collapsed. I prayed that the back torso shell would be fitted without a hitch, and it was. Since my sternum was cracked, they were also going to attach a neck brace that would help hold my head up. I had lost about 4 to 5 inches in height and my head was sitting on my shoulders. I didn't really have a neck at this point because of the neck compression fractures. The brace was going to take about five days to make. There would be some adjustments to make on the two straps that connected the front and back shell together to position them the most effectively to keep the brace tight against my body. Otherwise, what would be the point in wearing a brace that didn't do the job it was designed for? The good thing about this type of clam shell (brace) was that it could be adjusted to the change in my torso when I started to gain some weight back. That was the plan anyway.

The day they delivered the brace was eventful. I was told to sit on the side of the bed, and they would put the brace on me and make any adjustments needed. I realized there was some relief of my back pain after it was put on. I thought the clam shell would provide me enough relief so I could be more mobile and be able to do more walking. I was really tired of lying in bed. I couldn't wait to put the clam shell on and walk out in the hall. I walked in the main hallway for the first time in two and a half weeks. I'll be on oxygen for quite a while when I'm walking outside of my room. I don't care. I just want to get out of the room and move around. My Mum is nervous about my back. I can sense it in her voice when we talk about it. She wants the orthopedic doctors to check over my clam shell and see how they can minimize future compression fractures. From what she saw, I look like I'm always feeling pain in my back. And she's right. The pain is pretty constant.

I still had pneumonia because it had been resistant to penicillin, but my kidney functions had improved. My creatinine level is 1.9, which is quite a bit lower from where I started at 19.5. This indicates that the treatment for the myeloma is working and the numbers prove it. My shortness of breath and coughing were getting worse. My white count was elevated and I had a fever. So what else is new? At least my anemia was stable.

My weight is down to 144 pounds, probably because I've been on a liquid diet for so long. The problem right now is that the doctors don't know whether my deteriorating health is due to another infection or it's something else. More tests were ordered.

Chapter Five

MRSA

Dr. Lowe was concerned that I had something new going on in my body because the antibiotics weren't affecting whatever infection I had. I continued to have fevers and chills. Because of all the coughing, I've been very fatigued. I didn't realize how tired a person can get from coughing all day. I'm on ten different medications right now.

He called in an infectious disease doctor from another hospital, Dr. Hare, to determine what infection was stopping my progress. Lab technicians would come in at all different times of the day to draw blood. I shake my head now just thinking about it. They'd come in with their "tools of the trade" and start drawing blood from my arm. I'm surprised I had any left at this point, since they had taken so much already. Dr. Hare wanted my sputum tested, so I had to spit into a specimen cup and provide the lab with about two ounces. The sub-clavian catheter that was located over my right chest had been removed. I can see from looking at the area that it is swollen and discolored.

My team of doctors came in my room today for a consult, and as always, my family was in there to take notes and ask questions. The information can get a little technical, so the doctors would have to repeat what they had just explained. I think it worked out best for my family to be in the room because the doctors didn't have to go over the test results twice; everything was answered at one time when my family had the doctor's full attention. Hey, when you have five sisters that's what you're going to get. When you get me, you get them; it's a package deal.

They cultured the catheter and it came back positive. Now we know that this is the catheter that grew the MRSA and my sputum culture was positive for MRSA.

MRSA is a bacterial infection that entered my body through a catheter as it was used for kidney dialysis. In my case a weakened immune system was a contributing factor in contracting this infection. There are so many different types of this infection that you hope the doctors choose the right treatment. In my case, I was started on a treatment with intravenous Vancomycin, along with Rifampin and also given Levofloxacin to cover other possible nosocomial bacteria (infections that originate or occur in the hospital).

The MRSA bacterial infection is responsible for a large percentage of hospital acquired infections. It's bad PR for the word to get out that a patient in the hospital has contracted MRSA. People come to hospitals to get better, not get sicker due to the hospital environment. Since Dr. Hare came from another hospital it made for some interesting drama with the nursing staff. The infectious disease doctor recommended that my room be quarantined and that anybody coming in would have to wear a mask, gown, and gloves. There was a bright red sign on the outside of the door letting everyone know that I was off-limits to people wanting to just walk in my room.

The nurses were supposed to gown up every time they came in during their shift. They placed a small table outside my door which had hospital gowns, facemasks and rubber gloves. My Mum noticed that on several occasions the nurses would come out in the hall after they'd checked on me and angrily threw the gowns that they'd just worn for only a few minutes down in the laundry basket. Apparently they were peeved because these special precautions were taking up their time. The nurses believed that my whole room was infected with MRSA, so why should they have to gown up when it's already present? The infectious disease doctor wanted these precautions taken so those were the rules.

Whenever family or friends came into my room, they'd have to go through the whole routine with the gown, gloves, and facemask. I had to put on these items when I walked in the halls, which I tried to do three times a day. I also had to put them on whenever I would leave the room to go for a test or to get x-rays of my back and sternum. I remember seeing my Mum and Dad coming in to sit with me in the corner of my room near the window, reading or taking a nap with all those extra clothes on, God love'em.

If I appear depressed right now it's probably because I'm starting to understand what is actually happening to me. I think the meds that I'm on also have something to do with my mood. I'm more somber and I've lost some of my energy. It has been over a week since I was readmitted with MRSA. My blood cultures came back from the lab showing that after the treatment, the MRSA is under control and improving.

The respiratory therapist came in today to put the vibrator on my back. It's supposed to help loosen up the phlegm in my throat. I was using the spirometer to help loosen up the secretions in my lungs. The breathing exercises must have worked because I was coughing up a fair amount of sputum this morning.

Dr. Lowe's colleague is in today and says the sputum cultures show that the staph infection is still present in traces. So antibiotics are still important to fight the infection. My oncologists' colleague thinks the pneumonia will remain a good month, thus the doctors won't put me on any chemotherapy until the cultures and my x-rays show that the infection is one hundred percent cleaned up. When that is will depend on how well the antibiotics I'm taking for the pneumonia work.

Three people from Sue's church showed up to pray for me in the waiting area. There were other people in the waiting area already and they all joined hands and prayed, most didn't even know who I was. There were about 20 people in all. I didn't know that until Sue told me. Did it help? I think it did, and that's what counts.

At 5:30 Linda, the Registered Nurse (RN) who is taking care of me tonight, checks my blood sugar reading. It was 139, and therefore, I don't need insulin, yeah! The respiratory therapist came in today to train me on changing my breathing patterns. The doctors want me to take slow, deep breaths versus short, fast ones. The shorter ones are actually hyperventilating breaths for a normal breathing person. Consequently, I need to take slow, deep breaths. This session really tired me out. I did sodium bi-carbonate to break up the phlegm.

My big goal was to get outside in a wheelchair to get some fresh air. I was on oxygen all the time, so we needed to take the oxygen tank outside along with a pillow behind my back and pillows on both sides of me. My brother Tomas wheeled me outside on a sunny afternoon on the weekend, and he, my parents and a couple of my sisters sat under the umbrella at a table out in front of the main entrance area. We read the Sunday paper and watched people come and go along the sidewalk. I like coming outside, sitting under the umbrella, and watching the hospital staff moving around and hanging out on a sunny day. I planned on coming outside, to this part of the hospital as much as I could in the future when it's nice out. It felt good to get out of the hospital even for just a short time. My back was bothering me while I was sitting and the pain meds weren't really helping. I upped my milligram dosage. It helped.

Obviously, I couldn't walk, so the first thing I needed to do was stand up for short periods of time. If I could just walk in place...Wow! The first time I tried, it was a major struggle to even stand. I didn't have enough strength to maintain my balance and needed a walker to brace myself. But over time, little by little, I gained strength back by drinking protein shakes my family made for me. I'd have at least two a day. They had about 2000 calories in them since they were made with ice cream. My family was grilling me all the time about what I ate each day, and why I didn't eat more. Let's face it; hospital food leaves a lot to be desired. The food doesn't have much taste to it.

The only meal I always looked forward to was breakfast, because at least I liked what they had to choose from off the menu; scrambled eggs, pancakes, cereal, oatmeal, toast and the small containers of chocolate milk. I was able to choose my meal selections a week in advance, and I knew what was coming. I wasn't too excited about the process. I tried to eat a little bit of everything, even the vegetables. I had a system for the eating the vegetables. I'd stick as much of the vegetable as I would be eating for that meal one after another in my mouth. Once all the vegetables were gone from the plate, or my mouth was full, then I had to methodically chew and swallow. The food was already in my mouth. The sooner I started chewing and swallowing, the sooner I could be done. I hated eating beets most of all, but I deliberately ate them. They contain a lot of iron, which helps red blood cells. They're good for you, but they do taste awful. I thought I knew a lot about food and what was good for my body and what wasn't. But I continually learn more and more about what is beneficial and what is not when I am taking certain medications.

My condition is improving. I've been walking in my room with the help of a walker, and I'm still on oxygen all the time. The oxygen tube goes around my ears and into my nose. I can breathe oxygen in through the nose, which is the most efficient way to breathe. I breathe more through my mouth, which isn't the best way to get oxygen into the body.

My parish priest stopped by today to give me communion and say a prayer with me. I know it made my Mum happy having the priest visiting. My sisters were also very happy that I was able to whisper, sit up, and spit on my own.

I am going to be wearing the bi-pap mask all night. I'll have it on from right before I fall asleep (10:00-11:00 pm) to when I wake up in the morning (6:00-7:00 am). I don't know how I'll do with it, but it's what the pulmonologist is suggesting. We do what he recommends.

The weekend respiratory therapist came in for treatments, and I do pretty much what I've been doing the past few days. But I lucked out when my brother Tomas brings in some of his birthday cake. You can't go wrong with birthday cake in the hospital. The bi-pap is no more! I've been taken off it, which means that the treatment is going better. I have a humidifier for the bi-pap machine which I had on the 8th floor. The humidifier helps keep the mucous thin, which is a good idea for preventing another mucous plug. The purpose of nebulizer treatments is to open my air passage and allows me to cough up the mucous. The medication for the nebulizer is Albuterol. The solution goes in a small plastic container on the end of a hose. It looks like a peace pipe when everything is together. I'm breathing in the liquid solution that turns into vapor when the process happens with the help of the small machine which is attached to a hose. I'd say ten minutes after I start taking deep breaths, the Albuterol is gone and the treatment is over. I'm doing nebulizer treatments at all hours of the day and night.

Sleeping in the hospital is tough. I don't have any kind of sleeping pattern and don't get enough sleep. But in the hospital who does? And I have to be really tired and beat to take a nap. It doesn't help that the night time nurse takes my vitals (blood pressure, pulse and temperature) in the middle of the night, but it is what it is. I bite my lip and do it. I just had a nebulizer treatment at 4:50 am and a chest x-ray at 6:00 am. Lately I've been coughing up three to four tablespoons of sputum. I never realized how much mucous a person can have in their lungs!

I guess the doctors have a full schedule today, and that's why the chest x-rays are done at 6:00 am. They want to have the results when they make their morning rounds and can discuss the results with the patient. I'm eating breakfast for the first time in two weeks. My brother Tomas says it's the best birthday present he could ever receive.

My sister Trish and my brother Steve were with me for what they said seemed like a small task, but they knew it was one of many small steps that had to be done. They had been trying to get me to cough up any "small plugs" that were clogging my lungs. On my most recent chest x-ray these were tiny or smaller than a dime. My lungs were full of them and they were causing me to have crackly, labored breathing. The bacterium that was growing in the lungs was a symptom of pneumonia we were trying to avoid. The plan for the next few hours was to get the plugs out using a sitting position that didn't put too much pressure on my tender tailbone. That was a result of being laid up in bed for so long. They gave me ice water to drink, instructed me to take smaller coughs and then have one final big cough.

Sometimes there was a dime size plug, *a gift*, or so we thought. I'd cough until I needed a rest. This same scenario played out again and again in the next few days. For the next couple of weeks this was the same plan; clear the lungs and steer clear of pneumonia. As the days went on pain medications were increased to factor in changes in my bone pain. My family tried to make light of any situation. The doctors had given me a slower release morphine pump. I was pushing the button all the time. My brother Steve chimed in, "Hey guy slow down! Each bag is costing you about $200 a pop!" They all had a bit of a laugh from that scene.

Later that same day, I began hallucinating. I angrily ordered someone off the end of the bed that wasn't there. They remembered him as George, and he made a few appearances off and on while I was on 7th floor. Other times I asked them to turn the TV off and it wasn't even on. I was angry that they wouldn't follow my orders, even to the point of throwing something at the wall since they didn't understand what I wanted. Why would they? I was acting very bizarre at the time with all the medication I was taking. I didn't recall any of this happening later.

The nurses are prodding me to sit in the chair or the recliner whenever I can during the day. The chairs and the recliner are hard on my spine and sternum even when I use the clam shell to cushion the back and the seat. I've been on high dose morphine for the pain in my sternum and my spine. The problem is the doctor doesn't want me to be on high doses for very long, so they lower the dosage. I can handle the pain to a certain point but my mood changes for the worse when they reduce my morphine level. I would say my family notices it enough that they write it down in the day's notes.

As of this morning, I weigh 140 lbs. I haven't been at this weight since my sophomore year in high school. The respiratory, oncology, and pulmonology doctors come in for morning rounds. The doctors say I could leave in two to four days. I think it's going to be more like five to seven though. They talk about my progress and within a few minutes they're out the door and on to the next patient. At this point, I'm tired of the whole regimen, and I want to get the heck out of the hospital.

My physical therapist comes in three days a week to do some exercises for my arms and whatever else I can do. I get fatigued after five or six repetitions. I work with the same therapist for every session and she pushes me to increase the number of repetitions I do. I used to be able to do 50 – 100 repetitions of certain exercises. The pneumonia and everything else hit me a lot harder than I thought it would.

My family has been vigilant in keeping my room clean and disinfected. Whenever housekeeping is finished cleaning, my sisters or Mum would come through and clean wherever they thought needed disinfecting. I must have had the cleanest room in all the hospital, not just in the intermediate ICU. You couldn't tell them that it was already cleaned. They wanted it spotless, which they felt would help to keep me healthy enough to get out of the hospital. I'm already on two antibiotics for the pneumonia and the respiratory doctor is going to add a third. It's called Lanasal, which is to aid in the reduction of sputum.

My oncology doctor came in this afternoon and surprised me by saying I'd be released from intermediate ICU to a regular room on six east. I'll believe it when I see it. Visitors to my new room still have to gown up until testing shows three negative results for staph infection. I already have one down, two to go. Peggy and her daughter Rachel stayed overnight in the waiting area. Today, I'm giving another sputum culture for hopefully a second negative result. Visitors will still need to wear gloves after the third negative culture, because of my history of infections. That makes sense.

Peggy had a discussion yesterday with one of the nurses about taking the prescribed precautions while in my room. I think Peggy is adjusting to my being diagnosed better than most in my family. Her experience of being a social worker, helping her elderly clients over the years, and being in hospitals for regular periods of time, gives her the perspective that others may not experience.

My family has been diligent in reminding the nursing staff to wear gloves when they come in the room to check on me. If they don't wear gloves, someone in my family is going to remind them. No discussions, case closed. They wanted me to get better and ultimately be able to come home. It is always an uphill battle.

My family and I thought that if there were signs on my door about the sanitary precautions that had to be taken when entering my room that they would be followed by the staff. But I think that they need to slow down a little and think before entering every patient's room. They can ultimately affect how long a patient may be in the hospital.

When the nurses come in, a nursing assistant comes along to check up on me and observe. That's fine with me. I figure they can check me out that much quicker and then move on to the next patient. The sooner the better, as far as I'm concerned. I'm tired of being cooped up in this room!

It will take time to get acclimated to the brace, since it attempts to straighten me upright when I am in it. This is where the discomfort comes in. I need to start by alternately wearing it for a half hour and then taking it off for a few hours. The brace will cover the tip of the sternum to just above the top of my hips. The company who is designing the brace is aware of my fractured sternum.

There are other big improvements Dr. Lowe is seeing in my condition. My creatinine number now is 1.1, which is the lowest it has been since I was diagnosed. The creatinine numbers are a big testing indicator for myeloma patients. A nurse came in to give me a shot in my belly right in the middle of my dinner. My Dad wrote "dumb, dumb, dumb" in the daily journal. I think my family is really happy I'm out of the ICU. If anything, it shows them I'm back on track in getting better. They are working to get a bed like the one I had in the ICU, which can roll side to side and minimize the back pain.

My most recent tests show my protein levels are improving, which means a decreased chance of infections. The protein levels in my urine are down to 9,416, which is about half of what they were two weeks ago. But we want the number to be down to 0. My second sputum culture came back negative. The pulmonologist reported that one other form of bacteria was growing in my lungs, so they ordered antibiotics.

Today is Friday, and I'm going down to 3rd floor for a CT scan of my lungs. I need to be on oxygen and wheel it along with the IV stand when I go for the scan. We came up with a little brainstorm. I just put the oxygen stand between my legs in the wheelchair so we don't have to worry about getting the oxygen hoses entangled with the IV stand. I don't know if it was my idea or my Dad's, but I'm taking credit for it! I need to put pillows in my wheelchair for my back, and I take some short- acting morphine to help with the pain. I hope I don't end up waiting out in the hall in the wheelchair too long. It's happened before.

The company that designed my clam shell brace came in Saturday morning to check my measurements and make adjustments. They told me that whenever I was out of bed, I needed to wear it to support my spine.

Today, I had a little problem with the central line, which had been leaking fluid from my upper right arm. My sister Peg noticed that the line had fallen out and was lying on the bed. She mentioned it to the night nurse. She had to clean the area on the arm, and I needed to put on a clean gown. The bandage dressing also needed to be cleaned up and reapplied. It's just another bump in the road that I have to deal with in the hospital. Nothing major.

I started taking my chemo drugs again for the cancer. It's been about two months since I took it last, and trust me, I didn't miss taking it. The side effects are numbness in the feet and drowsiness. I don't have a problem with the drowsiness, just the numbness to my feet and ankles. My balance is affected because it's hard for me to feel when my feet touch the ground, so I get nervous about falling.

When you are a patient in the hospital for any length of time, your world becomes very small and revolves around the daily hospital activities. What is going on in the outside world seems miles away. You lose track of time and knowing which day of the week it is.

You can watch the news on TV and nothing seems as serious as what is going on with you in the hospital and your survival. There is no differentiation between day and night by the staff. When respiratory therapists have orders to give patients certain treatments, it doesn't matter if they wake you at 3:00 am to give you the treatment. The staff looks at what their duties are for the day and to heck with the patient. How many people want to be woken up at 6:00 am just to get weighed, only to go back to bed to try and sleep for another hour? Hospital staff needs to incorporate time management skills with their patient care, therefore patients can get longer stretches of uninterrupted sleep. That helps people heal.

The results from my latest CT scan show no change of the pneumonia in both lungs, which is not surprising. Pneumonia in both lungs isn't going to improve just like that. When my family gets news like this, they get even more concerned about my care. There are a lot of people looking out for my health. I'll never complain about that. Right now I'm more concerned about my lungs than my back.

The problem with my back is somewhere located along the line of the compression fractures, and the compressed vertebrae have worsened quickly. The strain on my bones caused my sternum to collapse, when I was admitted the second time for a bacterial infection, from an IV line. The turn of events has caused my family to worry even more. Me, I can only handle one thing at a time, and right now it's my lungs. Everything else has less importance.

Respiratory therapy came in on Saturday and put in a new tube. The last one had been lying on the floor and there are germs all over hospital rooms. Compromised immune systems can pick up infections very easily from those germs and set back your recovery for days or weeks. Some people never recover.

I've learned that when you go into the hospital for one thing you can develop other problems, either from the medications you are taking or from the environment you are in. I had a bad night with the mask and all the waking up and trying to get back to sleep. I have developed increased stomach acid and a yeast infection. As a result, I will have to add another medication to take, Ritalin. I don't care what it is as long as it works.

Taking short walks to the nurses' station has given me a little more activity and gets me out of my room. I need to get my leg muscles moving more, since I have lost most of my leg muscles due to inactivity. The walls in my room seem to be closing in on me at times. I need a change of scenery for my mental health. I usually walk with someone in my family or one of the nurses because of being unsteady on my feet. One of my pulmonology doctors is "amazed" that I'm walking as steady as I am. Is he talking about me?

My brother Tomas was in my room when I did a nebulizer treatment. He wanted me to cough quickly three times in one breath. This is better than coughing three times in three breaths, because mucous is pushed up at one breath. This type of breathing exercise produces good results in my case. It is amazing what you learn about your body when you are in the hospital. You have nothing else to focus on.

Since I still have the same bed I had in the Intermediate ICU (I lucked out) we continue to have my bed rotate side to side. I'm getting used to it now. Once the bed is turned on, it rotates at a 15 degree angle. The mattress is inflated like an inner tube to help with the pain in my back. I know it helps.

Sunday morning Sue stopped in with the newspaper. She and Mary tried in vain to hook up the VCR. That drove Julie nuts when she stopped by. I wasn't any help because I couldn't get up and see if I could figure it out. My back wouldn't allow it. We didn't get that VCR hooked up! It was much too confusing with all the wires and the hookups needed for the TV. The TV in my room is about nine feet off the ground, so Sue and Mary had to climb up and try and make it work. I give them an "A" for effort. Sometimes, it's the effort and thought that counts. I've been tired today.

With all the respiratory exercises, coughing, and walking I did today, I'm worn out. I just hope all that work makes a difference, but only time will tell. The protein shakes my family stashes in the fridge down the hallway help to put weight on. Chocolate shakes taste the best.

I am trying my best to do what I can to improve my health, with my diet, breathing exercises, and walking as much as I can. The rest is up to the doctors, medical staff and my family. Family plays a very important part of helping the patient recover. Not only are they your advocate but they bring you comfort and distract you from thinking about the hospital environment. They tell you about their families and daily activities. They know what your interests are and what you dislike. They can come in your room, read what kind of mood you are in, and have a conversation. Or they can say nothing at all and just sit there to let you know they are there for you. My family knows how much I hate to be in the hospital, so they arrange to have someone stay overnight in the family waiting area. They will come and check on me during the night to see if I am awake and whether I need anything. It is comforting to know that they are not far away. I am very fortunate to have such a caring family.

Dr. Lowe came in this morning on his rounds. He says my beta numbers are going down, which is a good sign. My sisters make a point to note the small changes in my health when they enter my room. On Monday afternoon, Peggy noticed the wastebasket was sitting on my oxygen line on the floor. Duhhh!" She wrote. "Who the heck did that?" If that happens and family doesn't notice it, then I need to make the nursing staff aware of it. I will ultimately be the one that gets the infection or have some other negative outcome.

Today I walked a little farther, but it isn't easy with all the precautions I needed to take. The walking helps my lungs, appetite, weight gain, and stress relief. I'm trying to work up to walking four times a day.

For now, I'm walking two times for about 10 minutes. I walk by the nurses' station, take a right past the waiting room, where my family sleeps at night, down the hall and then I walk back to my room. I have to look out for the food trays sitting outside rooms and the patients' machines being moved to make sure I don't bump into them with my IV pole. It takes some patience on my part, but where else am I going to go? This is the best I can do for right now. As long as I have a little hope for getting better, I can live with this for now. My Dad made an estimate that if I walk this path twice a day that I am walking about a quarter of a mile. That is a big deal for me since I was not able to walk out of my room at one point.

I'm just starting to take the medication thalidomide for the myeloma, which is going to have side effects. I had been taking a sleeping pill every night because of the restlessness I experienced. Dr. Lowe called my Mum and relayed that he doesn't want me to take my cancer medication with a sleeping pill, because of the side effects. This medication makes me real drowsy. Yeah! I don't need a sleeping pill anymore. Dr. Lowe mentions that I might get the feeding tube out in a couple days, which actually means five days. The neuropathy, *numbness*, in my feet is getting worse. Sometimes I don't know if I will stumble and fall when walking and ultimately do more damage to my bones.

Peggy is in to visit today. She took off my socks and rubbed my feet with aloe vera lotion to increase the blood flow and circulation. Is it working? Yeah! The problem is that all the rest of the time my feet are numb. I don't think the compression socks help me that much with the neuropathy. My Dad and Julie went for a walk with me in the halls this afternoon. No wait, it was more like a run. I'm starting to get some of my leg strength back.

Chapter Six

Visitors & Motivation

When I was diagnosed my Mum started to go to church daily and met with the priest to tell him about my diagnosis. She is a woman with strong faith. You could contribute money to the church and ask that masses could be said for specific people or causes. Mum paid for some masses, and in the weekly bulletin it is noted who the masses are being said for. The first Sunday that a mass was identified as being said for me, people started to ask my family members about me and if they could help in anyway. My friends were told that I would like them to visit, and others were told they could send me a card.

A couple of friends stopped in to visit today. I think that people were leery of seeing me because they did not know what to expect. But my family thought that it would lift my spirits to see some friends and let people know that I was up for visitors. Mike, a co-worker, was my first visitor. We caught up on what was going on at work. He filled me in on how people reacted when they found out I was diagnosed with cancer. They knew something was wrong with me but never thought it would be this serious. I'd always had a good relationship with people at work, and we did lots of kidding around, so Mike was a great person to see.

My college roommate Greg and his wife Brenda stopped in during the afternoon. They sat with me for awhile, which was nice. We just caught up, and I filled them in on where I am with my health. Greg didn't seem freaked out about my appearance. I am still pretty weak and the last time he saw me, I was 40 lbs. heavier and a lot healthier. It was good to see and talk with someone outside of my family and the hospital staff. Their visit was a definite morale booster.

Motivation is so important to keep you focused when you are going through devastating illnesses and treatments. My internal motivation came from years of training for sports.

I would automatically think each morning what I could do to exercise some parts of my body. It could be just walking in place next to my bed to get my legs moving. If you don't use your muscles you will lose them! I never gave up on my body. My sisters felt that I needed some external motivation to continue to push forward with the treatments. Either Julie or Mary brought in a photograph of my parent's house and the words, "The Goal" were written under it, meaning the goal was to get home. They taped it on the wall at the end of my bed. It did the trick, but I also had times where I would look at the picture and think about how long it had been since I was home.

Once the first picture was put on the wall, my sister Mary started to hang signs as reminders for anyone entering my room. The signs included "Wash your hands before touching anything in Tim's room", "Don't put Tim's plastic urinal bottle on his food table", " Make sure you put on gloves and mask before touching Tim", and "Make sure to clean under Tim's bed". It got to the point where the staff would look daily to see if there were any new signs put up. It was funny to see the staff's reaction to the signs.

My brother Tomas came in my room one day and said that laughter is the best medicine. So he brought in a tape of different types of laughs, which makes the listener start to laugh as well. Everyone in the room starting laughing and it felt good. He was right. It lifted my spirits.

My appetite decreased as I was taking my cancer drugs. My weight was not increasing while eating the hospital food. The hospital dietician wanted the nurses to record what percent of my food I would eat. I thought this was a little extreme but I'm not a dietician. I guess if I looked at my chart from where my weight was and everything else, I'd be concerned too.

The dietician spoke with me about my food choices and what I should be ordering on a daily basis to help me gain weight. Breakfast was the only meal I really liked to eat in the hospital.

Once the dietician talked to me and my family about my weight, my family started to ask me what I wanted them to bring me from outside restaurants. I liked Culver's food, so they would bring burgers and shakes from there. I also like pizza so they would bring me pizza slices from pizza parlors. Eating foods from the outside restaurants added a little bit of normalcy and variety to my day. Sometimes my family would eat with me, which was a change in my routine. Any changes in routine would kill the monotony of my day.

Another issue that my dietician talked about was that a side effect of the medications I was taking was constipation. One morning my breakfast tray showed up and there was prune juice on it. Now I know that I didn't order it because I hate it, so I figured out that my Mum was the one who marked it on my menu choices. She is always concerned that as a patient, you are not constipated, because you will always feel full and will not eat. I knew I had to buck up and drink it, so I pinched my nose closed and chugged it down. That prune juice provided the motivation for my body to empty my bowels, which helped to increase my appetite. My appetite began to increase and my family started to bring more burgers, shakes and pizza.

Chapter Seven

Therapy, Therapy, Therapy

Today I have a full schedule of physical therapy twice, occupational therapy once, and respiratory therapy every four hours. My door seemed like it was revolving all day. In between all these therapies I wanted to get my walking in. I'm using a walker to get around in the halls, though I need someone to walk next to me with the oxygen tank and IV pole. I'm getting more used to the walker every time I use it. I can't wait for the day when I can push the oxygen and IV pole on my own. I'll be a little more independent at that point, and feel that I have more control of my body.

When the occupational therapist came in, my sister Sue was there. They started to talk and they figured out that her husband was Sue's manager at work. It is a small world. The occupational therapist brought in a tool that was about 16 inches long and had a clamp at the bottom of it. At the top was a handle that I could squeeze and the bottom clamp could attach to things that I could pick up on the floor. This would minimize my having to bend over to pick things up, which would help minimize my back pain. The therapist didn't think there were any other tools she could provide that would help me.

The physical therapist's main goals were to assist me in strengthening all my muscles and building up my endurance. They had to be very careful though not to further injure any of my bones, since they were so brittle. I could tell they were apprehensive in working with me because they knew my skeletal system always hurt. I tried to push myself when working with them but I was physically exhausted when we were done with each session. I needed to rest and re-hydrate myself before my respiratory therapy session.

The respiratory therapist would use a vibrating machine on my back and chest to try and loosen up the phlegm in my lungs. The respiratory therapist had to be careful not to press too hard to further injure my bones. It always seemed like there was something in the way of reaping all the benefits of the therapies, and unfortunately it was my bones.

My family has noticed my mood has been more somber as of late. I don't know if it's the meds I'm taking, but maybe they are affecting my mood. I think as Dr. Lowe increases my medication dosage that I'm going to be more irritable, drowsy, and inattentive. These meds are strong, and I'm not even at the maximum dosage the doctor wants me at yet. I hope I can handle the side effects.

My picc line needs to be changed in my arm. Dr. Lowe explained to me that there are two main reasons to have a picc line inserted. The first is that the infusion medication would be diluted sooner since the opening is so close to a major vessel. The second reason, important in my case, is that the chance of infection from a picc line port is very small. Putting in a new picc line can either be an easy procedure or it can be a major headache. When the nurse pulls out the line, it feels like a piece of dried skin being peeled off my body. It's about the width of a piece of spaghetti and is about 12 inches long. I can tell how much experience the nurse has doing this procedure by how the process goes.

My primary pulmonologist came in to listen to my lungs today. He says they are "okay". What the heck does that mean? My lungs are either better or worse, they're not okay! My family is wondering why I need to be on oxygen at all. I'm on three liters now, and the nurse is going to turn it down to two. That is the lowest number you can be on oxygen.

Today, I had the physical therapy session from hell. My therapist wanted my full attention for this session. She shut off my IV machine. Does she think I can't follow a therapy session with my IV machine on? Just say what you want me to do, and let's get on with it. She doesn't know how far I will go to push myself. I just rolled my eyes and did what she wanted. I definitely paid for it after we were done, but that is what I had to do to increase my endurance.

I needed some fresh air after therapy, so my brother Tomas and Mary helped me put on my body brace, found a wheel chair I could use and put a couple of pillows on the seat because my butt is nothing but bones. It was a little windy, but I like feeling the breeze. My uncle Pat and his wife stopped by to visit while we are sitting out on the patio. I sometimes wonder what people think when they see me. I have lost so much weight, my hair is thinner, I am wearing a body brace and I am shorter. This damn disease has wreaked so much damage on my body that I wonder if I will ever have the stamina and endurance I once had as an athlete.

Even though I have therapists working with me, I control how many times I want to walk each day. This is one of the few things that I can control now. I try to walk at least three times a day and have started to add a little variety in where I walk. Sometimes I walk down to the children's ward or down the halls on the 6th floor. The nurses always say "hi" when we cross paths and I wonder what they think about all the walking I do. My goal is to walk 15 – 20 minutes each time.

The most recent sputum culture still showed signs of a staph infection. Man, I just can't beat these infections! I'm going to have a CAT scan of my lungs on Monday to see what benefits I am getting from the respiratory therapy and antibiotics. I am learning how much health care relies on statistics and images, such as lab numbers and x-rays, to measure internal progress of a patient.

Chapter Eight

A Scare

Mary calls me up and tells me she wants to ask me if it's all right to contact another hospital about taking over my case. She's worried Dr. Lowe doesn't have enough experience with my type of cancer. There have only been a few cases of this kind of cancer at this hospital, and nobody has seen a case like mine before. I didn't argue with her, but if she wants me to change to a different hospital or different medical team I won't do it. My doctors know too much about my case and have been persistent in dealing with all my setbacks to turn back now. I'll take my chances with this medical team until I don't feel that they have my best interests at heart.

Julie's notes-Mary makes contact with the Arkansas hospital when I have my mucous plug episode. This is my third episode with pneumonia. Julie says this is ridiculous. Mary makes a call to the scheduling nurse from the Arkansas hospital she met at the conference. She had already forwarded my medical records to the University Of Arkansas Medical Center Sciences Myeloma Institute for Research and Therapy (UAMS). Once Mary got a hold of the nurse on the phone, she explained what was happening with my health and the repeated pneumonia episodes. The nurse talked to the doctor they had met at the conference, to see if he had anything he could suggest to stop the repeated pneumonia episodes. They met this doctor while riding with him in a cab from the hotel to the conference they were attending. The doctor at the UAMS took a look at my case and recommended what could be changed in my treatment. We can't continue on with my treatments of the myeloma until we have my immune system under control. That wasn't going to happen with the pneumonia re-occurring.

Mary and Julie informed Dr. Lowe that they had contacted the doctors at UAMS and gave Dr. Lowe the name and phone number of the UAMS doctor they wanted him to contact. They were to discuss my case and provide a recommendation in my pulmonary treatment. Dr. Lowe consulted with the pulmonologists at my clinic and made a change to my medications. I am so thankful to my sisters, Dr. Lowe and the doctors at UAMS for thinking outside the box. We move on, it's about time!

My Mum took thank you treats to the 8th floor nurses, as well as the 7th floor IM-ICU nurses for taking care of me. I went in to take my shower and brought along my breathing tube, which I needed in order to be able to stand up and take a shower. For some reason, I am having a harder time breathing today and needed to sit down on a shower stool. I didn't know what was up. I finished showering and got out to dry off. WHAT THE HECK WAS GOING ON! Mary is out in my room blasting a U2 CD that she had just bought for me, so she is unaware of what is going on until I came out of the bathroom and was gasping for air. I barely made it to the side of the bed since I was so short of breath. I am freaking out, panicking. What is going on here? I feel like I am suffocating. She tried to calm me down and get me to take deep breathes. After a minute I slowly was getting enough oxygen to breathe through my nose. She went to turn up the oxygen level on the canister but it wasn't helping. What is going on here? We looked at the canister gage and the bottle is empty. How could this be when we just had a new canister replaced that morning when I was walking with Sue?

Evidently, when the nurse hooked up the tube to the canister she didn't check the level of the oxygen. And neither did we. We assumed there was enough in the bottle. The bottle was already empty.
I didn't have any oxygen probably the whole time I was in the shower.

We figured out that when we went walking earlier in the morning, Sue didn't turn off the valve on the oxygen canister after we finished walking and all the oxygen slowly leaked out throughout the day.

The night nurse felt so bad that she hadn't checked the amount of oxygen in the tank, which caused me to freak out. She leaves the room and starts crying. What I learned from that episode was that I and my family always have to double check things that affect my health. It was as much our fault for not checking the level in the canister as it was the nurse. This is where the team mentality comes in. Everyone has to back everyone else up and double check things. We quickly switched the tube onto the outlet on the wall that each room has and walla, no more problem. We had a good laugh about that story, but it wasn't funny to me at the time.

My lungs were slowly getting stronger. My lobbying to my respiratory doctor for switching to every other day on the C-PAP has paid off. Tonight's the first night in a loooong time I haven't had to wear it. It's hard to sleep when you have air being pushed into your nose and mouth at 30 miles per hour all night long. The CAT scan results show that I have slight improvement in my lungs. Well, that's something positive. I'm using between 1.5-2 liters of oxygen. At some point today, I received a "no oxygen assistance" status. You take the small victories when you can get them, and this is one of them. The notes my family takes from my pulmonary doctor's consults are getting smaller. Less writing means there's not as much to report about changes in my condition. I must be slowly getting better. I'm crossing my fingers. We'll see.

When I get my sleeping medication too late at night I feel like I have a sleep hangover in the morning. This morning I woke up at 9:00am, three hours later than I normally do. Time to make sure that the nurse gives me my sleeping pill between 9:00pm and 9:30pm.

Chapter Nine

A Ray of Hope

Another CAT scan was taken this morning, and the results showed my lungs were about the same. For the first time, my oncology doctor mentions I possibly could go home. He thinks that if I am at home I won't pick up as many infections as being in the hospital. He talks about possibly going home in 7-10 days. I think that means more like 2 weeks. I don't pay attention to the dates any more, just the days of the week. That's all that matters at this point. I need to improve on the amount of time I walk each day to get my stamina built up more before going home.

A lot of planning needs to be done before I can go home. A home health nurse needs to be scheduled to train my family in administering the IV infusions and medications I'll be taking. An oxygen concentrator needs to be ordered so I can be on oxygen anywhere in the house. We've been through this once so I think we'll handle it all right. I'm glad I have five sisters and my Mum to help with all the planning.

The pulmonologist was in today to explain that I'm being taken off two antibiotics. White blood cells are colonizing in my lungs. The white blood cells have detected a germ or bacteria in that area and have several ways to produce protective antibodies that will overpower the germ. The white blood cells also surround and devour the bacteria present. The only way my normal immune system can return is if I'm off the medications and the chemo drugs. Over the course of the next few days my labs came back and Dr. Lowe is "pleased" with them. I'm on "level 1" on the oxygen intake today. I will be so glad when I don't have to be on oxygen anymore. I'll love that day!

My hemoglobin is 9.9, optimum is 13. Hemoglobin is the main component of red blood cells. My body is producing fewer red blood cells than I need for my body to work right. My white blood cell count is normal.

Dr. Lowe has a meeting with my family in the waiting room to answer their questions about my discharge. For one thing the most recent x-rays show that pneumonia and staph infections are still present in my lungs. There are a lot of directions and questions that needed to be taken care of. My doctor put in an order with Home Health for a hospital bed like the one I had in the hospital, as well as other equipment that I'll possibly need at home. Dr. Lowe is very thorough in taking care of me. My Dad asked if I'm going to need oxygen at home. I think that will be determined day by day, but it's a good bet I'll at least have it on hand.

After dinner I go for a walk outside with the assistance of Julie and Mary. It's a beautiful night. Mary says she sees a big improvement in my walking from a week ago. I'm more sure- footed and hold my head up more now. Walking in the halls of the hospital is one thing, but walking out in public with confidence in my steps is another.

Dr. Lowe's partner, Dr. Frame, is very pleased with my progress. Dr. Frame covers for Dr. Lowe when he has a day off. My family gave Dr. Frame the nick-name Dr. Doom and Gloom. He gave my family the impression that he had already written me off for living very long because of all the health issues I had. He gives off negative vibes, which isn't very encouraging for someone who is trying their best to survive. He didn't realize my inner strength and how much family support I have. My Mum doesn't have the time of day for him.

Today is the first on many fronts. I've been off the c-pap for four days. I won't need it at all when I leave, yyyyeessss! I walked down past the nurses' station and took a right down the long hall and returned to my room without the walker. Today I went walking without oxygen. I'm a little winded at the end. I know it's going to take awhile before I can finish a walk and not be winded. I just need to be patient, it'll happen.

The physical therapist came in today and had a matter of fact talk with me. She was talking about psychotherapy. She mentioned men more often than women have a difficult time with feelings of anger and denial when they are ill. I would agree with that, however, in my case I'm not in denial. I know what's happening. My physical therapist wants me to see a psychotherapist to talk. My respiratory doctor has to write the order for the appointment to happen. The order is for the entire time during my rehab starting tomorrow. I don't know how this will go. I feel sarcastic about this, but I'll keep an open mind.

The meeting with the psychotherapist went more or less the way I thought it would. I didn't deny how I was feeling, and the psychotherapist didn't tell me how I was going to feel about my prognosis. I moved on and was thinking about getting discharged. I move forward, that's how I deal with having cancer.

I had a meeting this afternoon regarding my co-pays and the cost of medications when I go home. These are costs I should know about but that I don't want to know about. You know what I mean. It's the cost of survival.

My old college buddy Mike stopped by for a visit. He stayed for about three hours and we caught up with each other. He used to always bust my chops because of the high school I went to. He called the school I went to the "prairie dogs." I hated that name! He's one of those guys who never let you forget where you came from in comparison to where he came from. People do weird things.

When he left, he ran into my sister Peg out in the hallway, and she filled him in on my prognosis. Dr. Lowe wants to push ahead with my treatment. He's given us a list of what I'll be prescribed and where this treatment is going. I just hope my lungs improve first, so I don't end up back in here. This is a short term goal that I wish for.

This evening I watched an NFL football game. I prefer college, but I'll watch the pros if that is all that's on the TV. The Chicago Bears made a last minute comeback over the St. Louis Rams. I'm a Pittsburgh Steelers and Green Bay Packer fan, so I'd rather have seen the Rams win this game.

The following day I had a visit from the monsignor from my church parish. He talked about what was going on in the parish with the fall festival coming up and the rummage sale and this and that. He blessed me and he said he'd stop by in a week. I always like it when the monsignor stops by. It's like having the Pope visiting the hospital.

Dr. Lowe stopped by and said I looked good. During his visits he asks me how I'm feeling and shakes my hand and anyone else from my family in the room. He'd said I'd be going to physical therapy on the third floor. We're going to take a tour of the facility before I leave. I'm going to be on antibiotics for two more weeks as a precaution to prevent infections.

I walked with my brace today. I'm getting used to it. I sweat underneath the shell when I'm wearing it, but I don't need to use a walker any more. No IV stand, no oxygen bottle and hose!

The hospital food service is delivering my meals later than scheduled. The last two days my meals have been a couple of hours late. It is important to have my meals on time because when I take medications orally they should not be taken on an empty stomach. I cannot wait to get out of the hospital, I can't wait!

I've been walking outside the hospital as often as I can. I usually have someone from my family walk with me just in case I trip or something else happens. The fresh air helps me sleep better at night. It's a long way to travel to get outside. I take the elevator down five floors, then walk down the long main floor and go outside through the automatic revolving door.

Julie has been giving me massages for my feet. The neuropathy has been getting worse since my medication was increased. I think the massage is helping. Julie's really good at it. She's a massage therapist so she is very experienced. My fingers are tingling, but it's my feet that are really feeling numb from the medication.

My sisters are upset that the nursing staff is administering my pills at 8:30 instead of at 8:00: in the morning. They remind the nursing staff about giving my medications on time, otherwise it messes up my schedule for the rest of the day, as well as when my sleeping pill is administered at night. I'm thankful my sisters caught that and mentioned it to the staff. They've caught a lot of things since I've been in the hospital, and it's helped.

Chapter Ten

Discharged From the Hospital

My albumen level is currently at 3.1. It measures the level of protein in my diet. My level coming into the hospital was one point something, so I'm doing a good job and I need to keep eating like it's going out of style. The doctor will bump up my cancer medications another 50 milligrams sometime this week. Oh boy, I can't wait for the neuropathy to elevate even more in my feet and ankles! What a coincidence that the last page in this notebook journal is the last day I'm in the hospital. There are no coincidences. Do things happen for a reason?

August 23, 2002. Discharge day! It's about 7:30am and my breakfast is here. It's actually pretty good. I'm happy with the pancakes and milk. I know check-ins and check outs can stretch out over the course of a day, but to my surprise I was able to get out by 10:45 am. The first thing we did was go to a local restaurant called Culver's which has fat filling burgers known as "butter burgers," plus fries and milkshakes. I need to gain a lot of weigh back and this is the place to start.

I wanted to get outside as soon as I arrived back home, and Tomas walked with me down to the corner of the road and back, which is about a quarter of a mile. I knew my lungs were damaged from all the infections, pneumonia, MRSA and lying on my back for so long but I didn't think it would be this bad. The outside air and the humidity were a double whammy to my breathing and I had to stop walking a few times on the way back up the road to catch my breath. Still, I'm looking forward to uninterrupted nights of sleep. Man, I'm looking forward to that!!!

Living back home with my Mum and Dad has been an experience in itself, to say the least. They both have their routines during the course of a day that I didn't realize until I started being around them more.

63

My Dad, for instance, gets up early in the morning to read the paper. From my room downstairs, I can hear him when he wakes up and stands up when getting out of bed. When he comes downstairs the steps always creak. He wakes me up. My Dad walks flat-footed so his footsteps sound like a giant is taking steps as he walks out to the kitchen. He pours his cup of coffee, opens the microwave door, puts the cup in the microwave, slams the door shut and sets the timer for one minute. He walks out to the front of the house to look at the temperature gauge outside the front door. He doesn't just have one temperature gauge but two. I don't get that, but it's his house so he can do whatever makes him happy. When it's dark out he turns the light on in the front room. The light shines into my room. I am definitely awake now. He likes to check out the temperature gauge ALL THE TIME! That's one of his signature lines... "Let's see what the temperature says outside." He looks at the gauge at least five times a day, sometimes more. I think that is the farmer coming out in him.

Then he'll make a commotion putting on his winter coat that hangs up by the front door. He has an automatic start to his truck, so he starts it up right outside the door where it's parked next to the house. His truck has dual exhaust and makes a loud rumbling noise when it starts up. He'll let it warm up for a few minutes before he goes out. He takes his heated coffee cup out of the microwave and sets it on the table. If it's not too hot already, he'll start to slowly slurp the coffee. He's had this routine so long he doesn't even know what he's doing or how much noise he's making. Gosh it drives me crazy, but what am I going to do?

I'm already up and trying to get him to stop slurping his hot coffee. It's a lost cause, so I just sigh and laugh to myself. Dad will jump into his truck and drive up to the mailbox to get the morning paper.

He opens the patio door, which, to me sounds like its being slammed shut, and then he'll toss the paper on the table. Next, he'll take a drink of his coffee, making sure he slurps it, and then he'll take off his coat and hang it up on the hanger. Finally he'll come back to the table and sit down to take another slurp of his coffee and start leafing through the paper. I can hear him turn the pages. I'm up for the day. That's my Dad's morning routine and it will never change. I can set the clock by it.

I need to work up to the point of not needing to be on oxygen when I walk. It'll take quite awhile and a lot of patience, but I'm hoping my lungs will fully recover. I have an oxygen concentrator in my bedroom. The hose has two openings at the end where I can breathe in oxygen through my nose. I tend to breathe more through my mouth, so I need to work on breathing through my nose.

September 6, 2002. I've been home two weeks now. I was able to get a portable oxygen system to wear when I walk outside. I've been exercising with a physical therapist two times a week. She doesn't want me to use oxygen when I exercise with her, so I was breathing a little harder. It was exhausting at first. I can't stand her at times, but I know that what she is doing is just pushing me a little more each session. When I can't walk outside because of the weather (in the Midwest, give it 15 minutes and it'll change) I'd walk on the treadmill.

September 9, 2002. I'm spitting up some blood, but not from coughing. The nurse had stopped in earlier in the day and given me a shot of Procrit. I don't know if my coughing blood is a result from the shot or something else. So my Mum calls the doctor's office and explains what is happening, and it turns out that I'm scheduled to get the Procrit shot every two weeks, not every week. I think there was a breakdown in communication from the doctor's orders to the nurse administering my shot.

September 10, 2002. I walked outside on the road for the first time in a while. The humidity has been so bad and my lungs are still so weak that I didn't feel confident enough to walk down the road even with another person along.

September 11, 2002. Today, I walked about twice as far as I normally do. Mary and her husband Andy walked with me so I felt more confident to walk farther. Then my doctor called and said I can restrict my oxygen usage to when I exercise. Well, it's a start; little by little I'll be able to be on oxygen less and less.

September 12, 2002. I didn't sleep well last night for whatever reason. I rescheduled my physical therapy appointment for this morning because of my lack of sleep. Sue and her husband Lane came to fix my medication's container for every day of the week. It's a plastic container with all my medications separated in each day's compartment. All I need to do is to take out the meds for that particular day. It's a pretty slick operation, so even I can't mess it up. A nun from my church stopped by and gave me communion.

September 15, 2002. Mary booked a room on the seventh floor at the local Hilton Hotel to watch an Ironman competition. An Ironman competition consists of swimming, biking, and running a marathon. There are about 2000 competitors and the event starts at 7:00am on Sunday morning. Mary, my brother Tomas and I stayed in the room overnight and the next morning some of my siblings and nieces came to watch the competition with us. Our room faced the lake, which was perfect because the swimming portion of the event is first. It was a beautiful morning with the sun reflecting on the lake.

The athletes had to swim 2.4 miles in a course set up like a triangle. When the swim portion started, it looked like a swarm of bees moving in the water. The fastest swimmers were done in a little over 45 minutes. I was thinking can those athletes swim like fish! We stayed and watched the entire swimming portion and the part where the athletes began the bike portion of the race. The bike portion is 112 miles.

Tomas and I walked down to the ground floor at nine o'clock to watch the swimmers come out of the water and change from their wet suits into their biking clothes. They would run in the bathrooms as fast as they could to change and when they came out there was a line of volunteers that would lather up the athlete's arms, legs, and faces with sun screen. Then they would run to the bike area and find their bikes, in amongst 2000 bikes and start the bike portion of the race. We had to be checked out of the hotel by noon so we couldn't stay any longer. Besides, my back was getting sore from sleeping in a different bed and all the moving around. Competition has always been a good motivator for me. I liked the fact that I could get out of the house for a day; a change of routine does me good. We all had a great time.

September 17, 2002. I am short of breath this morning. I woke up several times last night to go to the bathroom. My temperature is elevated this morning to 100.7 degrees. I'm also showing blood in my sputum. That's not good. Mum called Dr. Lowe's office to give him my symptoms and see what he recommends.

The nurse called back and said I should come in and be admitted to the hospital. My Mum has some short-acting morphine pills for me to take to help with my bone pain, while the hospital does the paperwork to get me admitted.

I took the pills twice while I waited in the wheelchair. I think the fever and the soreness in my body made it seem a lot longer. In the end, I'm admitted at 12:15 pm to 6 East Wing and I arrived at 9:40 am.

Chapter Eleven

Bouncing Ball

I'll be in the hospital at least a week this time, while the doctors' figure out what's causing my temperature to elevate. I've taken a few steps back in my recovery. I just have to roll with it. My family worries enough for the both of us, believe me. I can't even keep track of what my diagnosis is this time. I feel like a bouncing ball, in and out of the hospital. But every time I have to go back in the hospital, I'm a little more demoralized in my confidence about getting better. Right now life is going forward for the world, and I'm bouncing back and forth.

September 25, 2002. Eight days later now and I was discharged yesterday. I'm back on my medication regime. I was treated for pneumonia again, put on antibiotics and the treatment helped lower my fever. My lab work was getting back to what it was before I was admitted. I have to take 10 pills of Dexamethazone (Dex) once a week and today is the day. I'm not looking forward to it. I take 25 pills over the course of the day once a week. I used to take the Dex all at once, but then I figured out that if I took some at the beginning of my meal and the rest at the end, my stomach can handle the pills better. It's trial and error sometimes.

The home nurse came to the house to give me an IV infusion, but she couldn't get the line unclogged and decided that both lines had clots on the end. She couldn't flush the lines. We called Dr. Lowe's colleague who suggested a peripheral line as a temporary method. We're going with that plan for the short term. I'm tired from the day's events and fall asleep as soon as my head hits the pillow.

September 26, 2002. The nurse arrives early to give me an infusion in the peripheral line, and the procedure goes off without a hitch. I'm glad and relieved. I gave my Mum a hand in making food for the upcoming fundraiser.

It kept me busy and my mind occupied. I hate beets but Mum has been cooking them a lot for me lately. There is a lot of iron in beets and Mum has been very careful about what she fixes for me to eat. She has attended some cancer caregiver meetings and they have talked about diet for people on chemotherapy. You can help minimize the side effects by eating the right foods. She has also purchased a couple of cancer cookbooks. These help her to know what's good and not good for me. Information is power. I eat the beets to make her happy. I stuff them in my mouth so I have to eat them and then I take my time chewing them. It takes a while to finally swallow the last little bit.

I didn't think I was going to get two infusions today, but evidently I am. The home health nurse arrives early in the evening. She can't get the line in so we phone the doctor on call and make a plan to go to the hospital tomorrow to hopefully get the picc line fixed.

September 27, 2002. I woke up early since we needed to go to radiology at the hospital to get my infusion line fixed. At the hospital I went to Seven Towers. The nurse tried to thread the line to the proper place, but the x-ray showed it wasn't successful. Great! If I didn't have bad luck I'd have no luck at all. As a result, we moved on to radiology to put in a new picc line. The second time is a charm; the x-ray shows the line is in. We left around 2:30 pm.

My Dad had been having pain in his lower abdomen for a few weeks and today the pain is elevated to the point where he needs to see a doctor about it now. My family decides to take him to the ER. They found he needs surgery for a hernia, so they perform the surgery today. He will stay overnight in the hospital and come home tomorrow. That is what they say happens to caregivers. He has been so busy taking care of me that he was neglecting his own health.

September 28, 2002. Today's the day of the fundraiser. The weather is nice for a change. My Mum goes to the hospital to pick up my Dad following surgery. I wasn't able to go to the fundraiser because my immune system was so bad, and we didn't want to take any chances with me being exposed to other people. My back and bone pain was so strong that I couldn't have tolerated being on my feet very long.

I know it takes a lot of time and energy to organize something like this and my family was up for the task. My sister Peg has lots of experience in fundraising, so she provided the guidance that was needed to make it a success. The fundraiser was held in front of a grocery store that I worked at part time prior to being diagnosed. The family that owns the grocery store had been very supportive of me and my family as we went through this journey. There was a band playing music, food and baked goods sold and some items were sold during a silent auction. The funds raised were used to help pay for my medications and hospital bills. You don't realize how much support you have until such an event is held. It was a big success and everyone in the family did a great job. They were all wiped out from the event. After a dinner of brats, fruit, and vegetables – a favorite meal of mine, I went for a walk with Julie.

September 29, 2002. My Dad administered my infusion this morning. The antibiotic he's using in the infusion is for the respiratory infection I've had in my lungs. He doesn't mess up at all when he does the infusion, so I don't worry. I wanted to walk outside today but the mosquitoes were bad. I haven't had any problems with taking my meds at night; I just have to be sure to take them on a daily schedule at the same time every night. The later I take them in the evening, the worse I sleep, so I need to follow a routine.

September 30, 2002. My feet are swollen more than usual today, due to the medication. The compression socks help, but not much. It's amazing how elastic our skin is. When you blow up like a balloon, due to swelling, and then it goes away, your skin does the same thing. Mary went for a walk with me. It was very warm out early in the evening (80 degrees) and humid. My breathing is labored when it's this humid. Sue and her husband Lane stopped by to watch the Monday Night Football game and I stayed up until almost the end of the game.

October 1, 2002. I get another infusion of antibiotics this morning. I'm going in for my weekly appointment to see Dr. Lowe. My feet and ankles are swollen. My weight is 147. I've gained 3 pounds since I was released a month and a half ago. In the afternoon I had a bone strengthening treatment that lasts two hours and we didn't get home until 5:00.

October 2, 2002. Once again I have an infusion early in the morning. I like to get it over with as soon as possible. Julie is here to spend the day, but we can't go outside since it is raining. My temperature is slightly elevated this morning; we'll keep an eye on it. I shouldn't have stayed up so late last night. Supper tonight was one of my favorites, fish sticks, a baked potato, and no beets!

October 3, 2002. I was still asleep when I received my infusion. That was great! The hospital called to say they'd be dropping off an oxygen concentrator, which provides more oxygen when turned up. The one I currently have delivers only three liters of oxygen at its max, and I was using more than that sometimes in the hospital. The new concentrator provides up to 5 liters.

My appetite has increased and I am eating a lot more food now. I'm only exercising for 10-15 minutes a day but it's a start. My sisters take me out for a ride once in a while to get me out of the house and get some fresh air.

October 8, 2002. I have a doctor's appointment today, so I'll be spending at least half a day in the hospital. I check in just before 1:00 and my labs are first. Dr. Lowe is out of the office until the end of the month, so I expect this appointment to go a little quicker with fewer questions. We get home at 5:45. Man I'm tired and so are my Mum and Dad. Who can blame them? Being caregivers is mentally draining.

Chapter Twelve

Result of Lack of Movement

October 9, 2002. Here we go again. I get my morning infusion and soon afterward my skin feels warm. My temperature is 99.9 degrees. We put cold compresses on my head and hope that helps the problem. Fifteen minutes later my temperature is 100.1. We called the clinic and they told me to take 650mg of Tylenol to help lower my temperature. I'm spitting up sputum with blood in it. At 10:30 my temp is 101.5. We call the doctor's nurse and she wants us to come in for urinalysis and blood cultures. I'm admitted to the hospital with a temperature of 99.7. I am assigned to the 6th floor, which is the oncology floor. The doctor prescribes Vancomycin and antibiotics. It turns out the spitting up of blood was caused by clots in both lungs. The clots are a result of my veins collapsing because I'm not getting up enough to walk around, due to my back pain. I was supposed to be getting up every hour and walking for even 5 minutes. It was my fault and it won't happen again. The doctor is putting me on heparin to thin my blood. The tricky part is getting the right amount of medication so my blood is at the right level.

October 10, 2002. The heparin seems to be making a big difference in just a day. Tomas wrote in the journal that I look a lot better and my breathing is good. The clotting could be a result of several factors including the pneumonia, the thalidomide, lack of activity or a combination of other factors. Dr. Lowe's colleague, who is on call and handling my case, believes that as long as the blood thinning agent is used, this is a controllable issue with heparin for the short term. We'll transition to Coumadin down the road.

I'm having an ultra- sound on my legs today to make sure there is no significant clotting in this area. The results should be available tomorrow.

The clotting and the pneumonia are probably not directly linked. The doctor's main concern is the treatment of the pneumonia and the staph infection, which is the major stumbling block for moving forward with other treatments, such as a bone marrow transplant or stem cell transplant to begin with. The antibiotics seem to be helping the pneumonia. I'm not coughing up any blood. The doctor advises to continue the current strategy to treat the pneumonia.

When you hear someone say you never get enough rest in the hospital, I now know why. The nursing staff has their daily list of items they need to complete for each patient and all they care about is checking off each item as it is completed. I don't know why but they would always wake me up at 6:00am to weigh me, instead of doing it when I am already awake. One of my sisters spoke to the staff and asked that the nurse that gives me my morning meds weigh me, since I don't have very many nights of solid sleep. It is not always about the patient when you are in the hospital.

I jumped on the scale and my weight is 150 lbs. My family has figured out where resources are on the 6th floor that we can use when I need something. If I wanted something to eat or drink in between meals, they found the kitchen and would get me some applesauce, chocolate pudding, a soda, or make me some toast. When I needed more pillows to support my back they found some extra pillows in the supply room and then they found where the clean laundry was kept to get some clean pillow cases. If I wanted to take a shower they would find a clean hospital gown and more towels and I would shower whenever I wanted and not bother the nursing staff. Mary and her husband Andy are going to stay with me for the night. Mary encourages me to cough and loosen up the sputum in my lungs. I fell asleep at 11pm and woke up at 7:30am, a good night's sleep. I seem to be more relaxed and able to sleep better when family is here with me.

October 11, 2002. I'm back in my room after having an ultrasound of my lungs and my Mum is here. I'm using five liters of oxygen, which is pretty high, but I'm only comfortable breathing at this level. Trish called and said she didn't even know I was re-admitted. Keeping everyone in a large family aware of what is going on with me daily is an undertaking. That's alright; I didn't want to make a big deal about it. I hope I'm not in here for more than a week. The blood draws showed that the heparin dosage needs to be increased as a precaution.

A different doctor stops in this morning around 9:00 to check on me. I think he's a pulmonologist. I can't keep the doctors straight now, meaning not knowing what kind of doctor they are. He says the blood clots can take up to three months to dissolve, which means I have something to worry about for possibly three months. He explains that the blood thinner almost entirely eliminates the risk of blood clots breaking off and moving from the legs to the lungs or somewhere else. The doctors are more concerned with clots in the legs than in the lungs. Blood has to travel farther to the legs and there is more that can go wrong having clots interrupting the flow of blood to the legs.

Trish and her family come to visit tonight. We fill out my menu and add a protein drink which can help me gain weight. It comes in a small can and you can drink it straight out of the can or mix it with something else like ice cream. A case of the protein drink costs around $50 for a month's supply, but it works, so it's worth it. Trish writes down in the journal that I've spit up four dime size blood sputum samples today so far, so the clots may be breaking up. She's pushing me to drink more water, but I can't. It ain't gonna happen. I'm ORDERED on bed rest by the doctors because they don't want the clots to move to other organs, like the heart and kidneys, and cause more serious problems.

I feel like I'm damned if I do and damned if I don't. I am supposed to get up and walk around for 5 minutes each hour so I don't get blood clots, but then I get blood clots and am told to stay in bed. So I will go to the bathroom one time and make it a good trip-brush my teeth, wash up, and then NO MOVING AROUND! The nurse listens to my lungs and says there is no wheezing or crackling like she heard last night. I have diminished breathing sounds in the lower lungs, especially the right lung. I'm hoping to get released in a few days, but it looks like I'll be here for more like five days.

October 12, 2002. I don't get it. I'm spitting up more blood, and the sputum looks more red than clear in consistency. Plus I'm on five liters of oxygen now. When I checked out of the hospital less than a month ago, I barely needed to be on oxygen at all.

I'm getting my picc line changed today. The doctors don't want to take any chances with the blood clots and me getting an infection from the picc line. I also had a culture of my sputum taken. My doctor wants to stay ahead of the game. He wants to make sure nothing out the ordinary shows up from the results, and if it does, he'll be prepared with a treatment protocol.

My college roommate Greg stopped in to see me again. I didn't think we'd sit down and visit under these circumstances, but life can be crazy sometimes.

I did get some good news. When I was first diagnosed, my cancer protein (creatinine), which is how Dr. Lowe measures how well my treatment is working, was 18.9 grams. When I left the hospital a month ago my number was nine grams and right now my number is three grams. It's down 80% since diagnosis and 33% since I left the hospital. The best number to have is 1.0 or less. The "cocktail" I'm taking is having a positive effect on the cancer. It's working! The dialysis I went through when I was first diagnosed helped flush the excess protein out of my system.

I had a CT scan which shows the lower lobes of both lungs do look better than when I left the hospital. So some progress has been made. The staph infection, however, has resurfaced again. Before I came in the pain in my side felt like a broken rib (which it wasn't) and blood in my sputum were early signals that the staph was coming back. This was partially due to our reducing the levels of the antibiotics, which is a necessary evil. The antibiotics must be reduced so as not to use up all their effectiveness. But the staph is a long term, very resistant, infection!

Dr. Lowe had to increase my antibiotic dosage now. The increase has already shown some results. My white cell blood count is down 20% in two days, which shows that antibiotics are working. My room has the red quarantine sign on the door again. The gowns, gloves, and face masks will be in place if my Mum has anything to say about it. I'm the one who pays the price if I'm exposed to something from visitors or staff. My Mum already questioned the pulmonologist as to why the staff wasn't wearing gowns and gloves. He said he was under the impression that it was already being done; however, he'll follow up with the staff today.

So now we have a table outside my room with gloves, gowns and face masks for anyone coming in. And if anyone including the hospital staff doesn't follow the doctor's orders, he'll hear about it from my Mum and sisters. I'm pretty sure about that.

I have developed a yeast infection in my mouth, which is called "thrush". The night nurse came in this evening to give me my meds and told me about a mouth rinse for my thrush. I will get it four times a day. I have to swish it around in my mouth for about five minutes and then swallow it. Also, one of my pulmonology doctors ordered a pill to help thin out the secretions, so it's easier for me to swallow and spit. I don't know what medications I am taking now for what, but all I know is that this is costing a boat load of money.

All summer I've slept on my back because of the pain, but last night I slept on my side for the first time in a long time, and it felt pretty good. The night nurse came in at midnight to do my vitals and I slept through it. Early the next morning, the nurse came in to draw blood and I slept through that too. I like it when I sleep through those procedures. Dr. Lowe's colleague came in around 9:00. He said I'm doing better, and it's the staph that's causing the bleeding. It's his opinion that the lungs are opening up and causing the bleeding. He talked about checking out home IV antibiotics and feels that the infections keep coming back because of being in the hospital. My family has resumed taking turns staying overnight at the hospital. When there is continuous turnover of staff my family wants to ensure that I am receiving consistent care and doctor's orders are being followed. They also continue to send out daily emails to all family so they can keep up on how I am doing. My brothers in Oregon have said numerous times how difficult it is living so far away and not being able to help with my care and help keep me motivated.

Chapter Thirteen

There's Not Enough Room

The pulmonologist came in and indicated that because my sternum is cracked that it is restricting how much my lungs can expand. Because there is not enough room for the lungs to expand, they are a breeding place for infections and it is more difficult to clear them up. He reinforced the importance of my blowing in the spirometer three or four times a day. I decided that going for a walk would also help my lungs. So I went for a walk outside and took it very slow. When I got back in my room and back in bed, I noticed that I had clean sheets on the bed. Thank you hospital staff!

I'm spitting sputum in the cup on my table. Dr. Lowe questions me about the sputum and examined the cup sample. When he listens to my lungs, he hears more "rattles." The nurse turned my oxygen all the way up to six liters. She wanted me to take deep breaths and to breathe through my nose rather than my mouth. My oxygen level was 89% before the breathing exercises. After 15 minutes, she tested me again and my level was 92%, which is acceptable.

Dr. Lowe must have felt that I was getting more fluid in my lungs, so he prescribed Lasix, which makes you urinate a lot. The nurse put it in my picc line. Wow! They weren't kidding about the Lasix working. I felt like I had peed out 6 gallons of fluids.

My college roommate Greg and his wife Brenda stopped by. It is good to see people other than just my family at times. I had no idea at the time but it turns out he was a major contributor to a fundraiser for me and also solicited contributions for the fundraiser. That was pretty cool! My sisters think he's one of my guardian angels. Funny but I just never pictured Greg being called a guardian angel. He could be called a lot of things but that's a new one. He's a guy who has a lot of energy for life and he doesn't mind using it to the fullest every day.

Mary stopped by to visit and to tell me about her work trip to Florida. While she was talking, I was doing my breathing exercises using the spirometer. I normally can get the yellow ball up to 1000 by blowing in the tube, but today I was moving it all the way up to the top. She reminded me that the first time I tried it in the ICU I could barely move the ball at all, so this breathing exercise shows a big difference now in my lungs.

The respiratory doctor came in today. She wanted to go over my chest x-rays with me. The x-rays show there's been no improvement in my lungs. In fact, the right side looks a little worse. This is not good to hear. They're considering putting me back on the c-pap. I don't want to go back on that! I really need to walk and do the deep breathing spirometer every hour. The doctor will re-evaluate whether we should start the c-pap after I do these exercises. I hope this condition is just a blip on the screen. My next chest x-ray is coming up on Monday so I'm going to be diligent about these exercises.

Mary mentioned the c-pap and I went walking, I didn't want to hear about it. I walked three times around the hospital wing on four liters of oxygen, which is getting pretty high. My oxygen during the walk measured 97%. I'm doing everything I can with the nebulizer, spirometer, walking, percussion therapy and breathing through my nose so I wouldn't have to put the C-pap on at night. You name it, I was doing it. But not having enough room to expand my lungs to their fullest was still an issue that could not be addressed at this time.

My latest breathing problems have raised new questions. What is the short- term plan regarding my cancer treatment? Will my original infectious disease doctor be called in to consult on the staph infection? These and several other questions are being brought up by my family, which is good. You have to look at the big picture with so much going on. And with all this in mind, the doctors decide that the first priority is to get the staph and pneumonia under control.

Whenever he stops by, my brother Tomas likes to push me to exercise and drink a lot of water. Today is no different. I walk with my oxygen on four liters at a pretty good pace. The walking increases my need for liquids, so I drink more water. The walking helps me to sleep better at night, which is another reason I do it. I also have a weakness for chocolate chip cookies. I love to dunk them in a small carton of milk the hospital gives to patients with their meals. I know they are not the healthiest food for me to eat but I'll take whatever pleasures I can for now. When I don't get enough to eat when my food tray shows up I have my family bring me something. I like chocolate shakes and hamburgers. Today, I had a fruit parfait. It tasted really good.

Sunday morning my oncology doctor's colleague gives me an update on my health. The treatment is going well, he says and he would anticipate me going home Monday or Tuesday, depending on the results of my Monday morning chest x-ray. I hope it comes back looking good. I'm already tired of this place.

Now it's Monday afternoon, and Julie stops by to visit and accompany me for a walk outside. We walked three laps in the cool temperatures with the oxygen at five liters. It is windy, so we don't stay outside and sit.

My latest tests show no more abnormalities in my liver functioning due to certain meds I was taking. I think that these test results show that the staph infection is causing the pneumonia and the doctors seem to agree.

My family is being trained and educated on how to administer the infusion of antibiotics after I go home. My Mum and my sister Peg will be training tomorrow morning. My Mum is the most worried about making a mistake. My pulmonary doctor came in for a visit today. He says the x-ray was the same as three days ago. The right lobe is more closed than open on the x-ray, but all the other things are better. He says it doesn't make sense because the lungs sound better.

My Dad is in this evening. He writes in the notes how far the hallway is and how many total feet I walked. Yeah, that's a military note- taker right there. I had Julie bring me a thick slice of pizza I was craving for. I took two bites and was full. I'll save the rest for when I have a meal that doesn't fill me up.

I'm still walking on four liters of oxygen and sometimes five liters. My breathing is not going to be noticeably better until I drop down those numbers. The last time I was here I was hardly using oxygen to walk in the hallway. I had labs today. My oncology doctor wanted to see what my CR-protein (myeloma numbers) are at the moment. The labs came back and the myeloma is now at 2500. That's alright compared to where I was at the beginning, but he wants to see it go below 1200.

One side effect of taking Dexamethazone (steroids) is that it elevates the white blood cells, which makes you more susceptible to infections like I've had. Am I more at risk of getting an infection with the picc line being in so long? The nurse indicated that infections are more prevalent in ports put in the chest.

I've been taking short acting morphine for my back. I want to cut the dosage in half because my back has been feeling better. I think wearing the brace is helping. The nurse didn't want to completely cut out the morphine because I'd have abdominal discomfort if I did. I haven't been too hungry the last few days and have been lethargic, probably because of the meds I'm currently on. At least I hope that's what it is. I'm just trying to stay as active as I can, walking in the halls or outside. I'm trying to sit in my hospital recliner as much as I can as well, which at least gets me out of the hospital bed.

October 17, 2002. I'm going home today. I'll have a week until I need to come in for another appointment. If everything goes well with that appointment, I won't have to be back for a check-up for another three to four weeks. The discharge is at 10:45 am, and we head to Culver's for lunch. No more hospital food!

After lunch, I want to walk with Tomas to the end of our block, which is a couple hundred yards. It's really humid today. My breathing is labored and I have to stop a couple times to catch my breath. I should be walking with portable oxygen, but I screwed up, thinking my lungs could handle the fresh air and humidity.

It's good to be home. I get to watch ESPN again. I only weigh 143 lbs. I gained some weight back while I was in the hospital, but I really need some of my Mum's home cooked meals.

I'm gaining some weight back and my clamshell brace is getting pretty tight on the sides. Mary calls to have the technician show up to make alterations. My picc line was changed a week ago, and it'll be changed again this Friday. Dr. Lowe doesn't want any chances of an infection from the line. It's not a big a deal to me anyway. I just want to get it over with and get the line changed so the antibiotics can be safely to put through by my family at home.

Julie, Peg, Mary, Sue and my Dad are watching a video about administering one of my antibiotics. Now that I'm home, I need to get up every hour to walk around. I just keep my brace on all the time because I don't want to have to keep putting it back on. It is difficult to put on and off because of my bone pain. Around 4:00, I went on the treadmill for 25 minutes. I ate some leftover spaghetti my Mum made. I could eat my Mum's spaghetti seven days a week.

October 20, 2002. It's Saturday, I was going to go shopping with Mary but she decided against it. My ankles were too swollen, so we went back to her house and watched the Wisconsin Badgers football game. Did I tell you I'm a college football fanatic? I can watch college football all day. Mary called the doctor on call about the swelling, and he said I should keep my feet elevated and get up and walk (not stand) every hour to prevent clotting of my blood.

Julie came today to give me my IV of Vancomycin. She also brought along a new winter coat and shoes for me. My old winter boots don't fit because my feet are so swollen. Wow! I look at the daily medication's list my Mum made out. I'm taking 25 pills a day. Can the human digestive system really handle that many pills? I don't think so.

October 22, 2002. I have a check up today. My Mum, Dad and Peg are in the room. The lab does the blood draws as usual but I never watch this. The appointment with Dr. Lowe begins before my labs are given to him. I'm still susceptible to bacterial infections. My blood count may be okay, but still susceptible because of the cancer.

I make myself walk as much as I can and try to get on the treadmill every day. I know the walking helps my lungs, but I still need to be on three liters of oxygen when I walk. My Dad rigged a system for my oxygen hose. He put a nail above my door so the line wouldn't be on the floor. The line runs around the nail from the oxygen machine out into the living room and into the TV room where I sit. The hose has to be about 25 feet long. I've grown accustomed to winding it up as I move around. The important thing is that the nose piece does not to touch the ground whenever I take it off or else we have to replace it. The home health nurse came today to take out the picc line. My weight has dropped about 12 lbs since my last weight check. I don't know what that's all about, because I'm eating well. Later, I filled out thank-you notes to people who donated at the fundraiser.

Chapter Fourteen

Continued Generosity

October 24, 2002. My sister Sue has been managing my finances and she had a discussion with the rest of the family about my expenses. I was not going to be eligible for disability payments until January and my funds were getting used up quickly in paying for medications and hospital bills. They decided to have another fundraiser at an area brewery with an outdoor stage for a band. I'm hoping the weather is going to be nice and it turned out to be gorgeous weather. There was a lot of food, a rock band, a disc jockey, and a lot of silent auction items for sale. One of my sisters had bright yellow t-shirts made with printing on them that said "Cancer Sucks". All my siblings, nieces, nephews, and parents wore the same shirts. You could definitely tell who my biggest supporters were that day.

My family had a silent auction, and the highest- priced item was a green- and- white football autographed by Brett Favre. It went to a local businessman who had really wanted that football. The bid sheet for the ball was set on the bar inside the building, and he sat at the end of the bar watching people come in to put in their bids. Whenever someone bid higher he always raised his bid, until it came down to him and another lady, and he outbid her for the ball. My Mum even had a part in the football auction. She found a local engraving company who gave her a clear plastic case for the ball so it wouldn't collect any dust while it sat on the shelf. My brother Scott set up all the sponsors for the event, and he had a banner with all their names outside on the chain link fence as you entered the brewery.

The DJ played the song "We Are Family" and all my family members went up by the stage and danced. It was fun to watch them. Our family loves to dance.

The turnout of people was amazing and everyone gave me words of encouragement. A lot of people paid double for food as a donation. The family ended up raising $11,000. Just incredible! I couldn't believe how much money people had donated. I'm writing out thank- you notes to everyone. This is going to take awhile. God love my family for putting on a great fundraiser AGAIN! As I have been going through this journey I am seeing each of the gifts my family members have and was not aware of before.

November 3, 2002. Today is Saturday, not a good day. I've been quiet, tired and irritable. Sue noticed I've become this way in the afternoons and into the evenings. Mum asked me why I'm unmotivated to do much exercise and I don't have an answer for it. Sue noted that on Saturdays when I take the Dex my mood and focus starts to change.

Here is a weird thing that happened. My Mum took me over to Sue's house and I would either walk around or stand in the same spot for five minutes, stare at one object, not answer to my name, then move to another spot and do it all over again. Trish asked me what I was doing and I said, "Nothing, I'm fine." I did the same thing at home last night. I stared at the nieces' and nephew's pictures on the refrigerator for about 10 minutes. Then I moved to different places in the kitchen and stared. Since this was not normal behavior for me Mum figured it was the medications and contacted the doctor to change the dosage of the medications for depression.

With my recent respiratory infections, I would take short trips to get out of the house. It wasn't wise for me to be around groups of people and risk picking up another bug. Sue sometimes drove me in to get some ice cream at the Dairy Queen and I would stay in the car while she went in and to buy a couple of cones. Another time she drove me down the road to see some new huge grain bins being built. I know, really exciting stuff. But it's best for my lungs that I am only exposed to a few people.

The home health phlebotomist came to the house for a blood draw, but no luck. My veins were rolling again and we'll have to wait on the blood draw until my next doctor's appointment. I've been walking on the treadmill religiously every day. I keep my sanity by walking.

Dr. Lowe is ordering compression stockings for me. They are supposed to help with the swelling in my feet, which is pretty bad. My appetite has been good. The routine of walking works for me. So I'll keep doing it. I'm keeping my feet elevated above my heart in the recliner as much as I can to help with the swelling.

My weight is up to 168 pounds now. The exercise, the meals my Mum makes, and a good night's sleep is doing the trick. I really like eating Kentucky Fried Chicken meals. It tastes good just writing about it.

I can only lift 5-lb weights for weight training, so I do what physical therapy says.... for now. Within the next month I need to take a breathing test to see if my lung capacity has improved enough so I could handle a possible bone marrow or stem cell transplant. Having a goal to strive for gives me more motivation to do whatever I can to make it happen.

Chapter Fifteen

Walk, Exercise, Breath

I went over to Mary's to watch a college football game and we went walking outside. The temperature was only in the forties. When I am walking outside it really tires me out. It's totally different than walking on the treadmill. I can't believe the outside air affects my lungs so much but it does. I'm glad Mary is along in case I become short of breath.

November 4, 2002. Mary, Julie and my college buddy Greg came on Sunday to watch the Packer game against the Miami Dolphins. I'm a Packer fan, but I'm also a huge Pittsburgh Steelers' fan. I feel I have the best of both worlds. Being able to watch football games is awesome. When I was in the hospital they did not carry the television channels that broadcast the games I wanted to watch. It would have helped to keep my mind off the daily routine of being in the hospital.

Today I graduated to eating at the family dinner table with my parents. Up until this point Mum would bring me a tray with my meals on it and I would sit in the recliner because of the support it provided my back. With my brace on and taking the pain medications I am able to sit up longer in a regular chair. We are taking baby steps forward.

The doctors had been focusing on all my infections and the cancer since my diagnosis. I, on the other hand, also had to deal with the compression fractures and the pain in my back. Anyway, I hope to find a solution to fix the problems with my back. I'm going to explore that whether the doctors like it or not. They have their agenda and I have mine.

My sisters also wanted the doctors to focus on my skeletal structure, since the damage from the cancer was causing me a lot of pain. I had lost 4 inches of my height and my head was literally sitting on my shoulders. I looked like I didn't have a neck and I could not stand straight up.

The sisters talked with Dr. Lowe about my skeletal system and whether there was something that could help strengthen my bones and slow down any further damage from the cancer. He indicated that there is a bone strengthening drug called Zomata I could try. He had given it to elderly myeloma patients because their bones were brittle to begin with and the myeloma further compromised their bones.

But I was his youngest patient and sometimes you need to prod the doctor to think outside the box when designing treatment plans, which my sisters did. Zomata is given through an IV once a month. The possible side effects are flu-like symptoms, achy joints, queasy stomach, and fever. But I've handled most medications pretty well, so I'm crossing my fingers. The side effects could last up to three days. We also asked how you can tell if the drug is working and Dr. Lowe indicated that a baseline skeletal x-ray is taken before administering the drug and then another skeletal x-ray is taken between nine and twelve months after taking the drug monthly. A comparison of the two x-rays is done to determine if there are benefits gained from the drug and if so, Dr. Lowe would continue to prescribe it. We were taking a few more steps forward as far as I was concerned.

November 17, 2002. I'm outside walking freely now without the use of oxygen. I have to wear the brace but at least I'm able to be a little more independent. I'm also off the oxygen at night. I don't know who is happier, me or my Dad, who doesn't have to put that damn c-pap mask on me anymore at night!

Relative to my lungs, Dr. Lowe and the pulmonologist want to do a new procedure called a pulmonary function test, which measures if the lungs can use a good volume of air and exchange the air through the blood stream. The test reveals how strong the lungs are to pump air for various levels of activity and also checks to see if the lungs can exchange gases.

The purpose for completing the test is to determine if I could go through a bone marrow or stem cell transplant and have adequate respiratory functionality to make it through successfully. The process for gathering the data is as follows: I would be placed in an enclosed "bubble", which controls the levels of oxygen around me. Monitors are hooked up to me and then I am asked to take deep breaths and then exhale as much air as possible into a machine that measures the amount of oxygen I produce. To pass the test I needed to attain at least 51 percent capacity. I was really motivated to increase my lung capacity.

I had not ever received a personal call at home from Dr. Lowe until today. I had initially thought something was wrong with my lab results, but I learned just the opposite. The results from the 24- hour urine collection reveal my protein level is 512, down from 1395 one month ago. I can imagine my sisters jumping up and down when they heard these results. The lab work also showed my numbers for anemia were elevated. The solution is to increase the iron input in my diet. More beets!

Since the last time I saw the home health nurse, I've picked up a chest cold. The home health nurse heard only a few crackles in my left lobe. And the way to fix that is to keep doing what I've been doing- the nebulizer treatment along with blowing into the spirometer at least four times a day, and walking outside when the temperature allows it. I walk up and back on our gravel driveway. This way I don't have to deal with traffic on the road. I'm not too confident walking on the road alone wearing a brace.

It is Monday and the physical therapist is coming today and she is the physical therapist from hell! My legs are weak and I only have a fraction of the muscles that I had in my legs. She doesn't care. I want to kick it in gear and show her what I can do. I don't know if she's trying to motivate me by pissing me off, but it is working.

She suggested I wear my brace even while I'm sitting and showed my parents how to put it on while I am still lying in bed. The orthopedic doctor feels that with my compression fractures that putting the brace on before getting out of bed would safeguard my back bones. I'm not too happy about that. It needs to be snug to work properly and with my sternum collapsed it presses against my lungs. I suppose I'm going to be a compliant patient, after all, she is not doing this to be mean, or is she? I get to spend time with her three times a week. I can hardly wait until Wednesday. The home health nurse also stopped by and gave me a shot of Procrit for stimulating red blood cell growth, which stimulates bone marrow. It is given once a week. I feel like I am moving in a more positive direction now in preparing for a bone marrow transplant.

Mary brought some movie videos and walked with me down to the corner after her work day. My sisters have all been stopping in on different days after work to see how I am doing and to help my parents.

I'm back wearing the c-pap at night along with doing the four nebulizer treatments a day. I think Dr. Lowe and the pulmonologist feel that since my lung issues are less at the moment that they want to keep it that way and not jeopardize moving forward with the transplant.

It's Saturday and Tomas is going on a walk on the country road with me today. It's a good day for a morning walk. The sun is out and it is not too cool. My breathing was a lot better this time so my lungs must be improving.

I need to improve my muscle strength in my legs, which walking helps with. College football season is my favorite time of the year. I always like it when my siblings come out to visit and watch some games with me. Today, my brother-in-law, Lane took me to Dairy Queen for ice cream. It felt good to get out of the house and have a few laughs with him.

It's Monday and the parish monsignor stopped by to give me communion. We visited and he blessed me before he left. I'm a believer and it always lifted my spirits when he came by. My physical therapist was a no show today but I did my exercises anyway. Scott stopped out to walk with me and instead we watched an NFL game.

It's Tuesday and I had an upset stomach and my physical therapist is scheduled to stop for an appointment. So, I can't remember whether I really had a stomach ache or I made it up to get out of having the therapy session. So we called and cancelled. I find it strange that from my Mum's handwriting in the journal notes for today that I had a bowel movement. Only my Mum would write that down. But she realizes how important it is to have all my body systems functioning correctly.

I'm walking more on the treadmill now since the weather is getting colder outside. I walk for at least 20 minutes at a time. I raised the incline on the treadmill since it was boring just walking on a flat surface. I want to be able to raise the incline to its highest level; that's my goal down the road. With the increase in my activity came the increase in my appetite. My Mum makes me a variety of meals to eat but always asks if something sounds good to me before she makes it, since my taste buds have changed.

She always includes one kind of vegetable at lunch or dinner. She can make anything taste good. This is one of her most important contributions to helping me build my body back up.

And when I was used to exercising everyday and then all of a sudden I had no activity at all, you can imagine how my stamina went in the tank and I lost most of my muscle mass in my arms and legs.

We found out after the fact that I was supposed to get the Procrit injection every other week, not every week. I began spitting up some blood soon after I received my most recent shot from the home health nurse. We called Dr. Lowe and told him the symptoms and he said I should have been getting the shot every other week to begin with, not every week. Communication was the issue. I hope that's the end of my spitting up blood.

Today is Wednesday and I walked in the early evening about a mile, which is a long distance for me. As always I wore the clam shell brace. Mary and Andy walked with me to make sure I didn't fall in the ditch on the side of the road. My Mum and Dad don't trust me to walk by myself on the road. I don't trust myself walking alone anywhere right now either.

My mindset at this point was that I needed to exercise as much as I could and use things around the house to assist me. I would stand at the kitchen counter doing exercises so I could use the counter to brace myself. I also used a kitchen chair for some of my exercises. I was doing standing squats, trying to go down as far as I could, which is only about a quarter of the way with the brace on. By the time I am done doing the squats, I'm breathing hard and I'm sweating up a storm. I'm bushed from doing just the squats and climbing four stairs up and down. I sat down to catch my breath and take a break. I had enough exercising for the day. Obviously, building my stamina back up is going to take longer than I thought. I received communion at the house today from one of the nuns from my parish. Fridays are going to be the appointed days for me to get communion. I can't go to church yet so this is the next best thing for me now.

Chapter Sixteen

Moving Backwards

I peed a lot during the night. My Mum's words in the journal were I "urinated a lot during the night". I had shortness of breath and my temperature was 100.7, so my Mum called the oncology clinic and she left a message for Dr. Lowe, who was otherwise detained with another patient. Then the nurse called back and said I should be admitted. Man I hate this! The doctor needs to find what is causing my shortness of breath, frequent urination, and my temperature.

When we arrived at the hospital I was feeling weak, was very pale, and my breathing was labored. If my Mum hadn't brought my meds along, I wouldn't have gotten anything for the pain in my back while we waited. Thanks Mum!

Dr. Lowe was surprised that Mum brought me in and that she made the right call in bringing me in, she knew something was wrong. I was admitted to the 6th East floor. This was the floor where I have spent the majority of my hospital stays so far so many of the nurses knew me from being there before. I liked all the nurses on the sixth floor, unless they were the ones waking me up early every morning to get a weight check. I guess it could be worse I could be in isolation. I lucked out in that they were able to move me down the hall to a bigger room with a better view of the downtown campus. One of the reasons I was moved to a bigger room at the end of the hall was because my family was so big and they didn't want the rest of the patients disturbed by the number of visitors I would have. Two days after I had an ultrasound, Dr. Lowe said I had blood clots in my lungs and developed lung infection-again.

He immediately put me on strong antibiotics, at the same time being concerned about me becoming antibiotic resistant at some point, since I had been on so many antibiotics before. Coumadin, a blood thinner, is going to be used to break up the clots.

The phlebotomist came in my room every four hours to draw blood so they could get the dosage of Coumadin right. My diet had to change because of being on that drug. I couldn't have any green leafy vegetables because they affected my INR, which is a number the doctors monitor when you are on Coumadin.

Someone sent flowers to me and after about 2 hours I started to get a really bad headache. We figured out that the flowers were bothering me and we got rid of them. Flowers never used to bother me but since I have been on so many medications my sense of smell and taste have changed. Some of my favorite foods were no longer my favorites.

The antibiotics I was taking for the infection worked. I was breathing easier and I didn't have as many clots in my lungs. I was discharged after 8 loooooong days in the hospital. I'm getting to hate this hospital!

I'm going to watch a football game with my college roommate Greg tonight. When I watch football it keeps my mind busy analyzing what is happening during the game. I observe what each team is trying to do in order to win the game. This is why I don't comment on every play like my Dad does, it takes too much effort over the course of a whole game. I want to enjoy the game, not suffer through it. I get to not think about my condition for three hours when I watch a game. I enjoy games now more than ever. Tonight one of my favorite teams plays on Monday night football, the Green Bay Packers versus the Chicago Bears.

The holidays were a blur, but at least I was able to be home during this time. The highlight of Christmas was seeing my brother Steve dressed up as Santa Claus and carrying his bag of presents through my parent's front door.

February 18, 2003. Three months later and we met with the pulmonary function doctor. He says the same thing about my lungs I've heard before, over time they'll heal. I need to be patient.

I'm feeling healthier, although it doesn't sound like it. In a couple months, if I can stay healthy, Dr. Lowe will consider a bone marrow or stem cell transplant. All my siblings have been tested to see if anyone matches me for a bone marrow transplant. You'd think with nine brothers and sisters that I'd have a good chance to match someone in my family.

Dr. Lowe called me in for a consult, which is strange since he's never called me in for an unscheduled appointment before. I think I know what it's about but I'm going to wait and see. My Mum and Dad go with me into a meeting room and sit down while Dr. Lowe explains that I didn't match anybody in my family for bone marrow. That's scary, what do I do now? But Dr. Lowe isn't too disappointed. He said that in my case a bone marrow transplant would be too dangerous. A stem cell transplant, using my own stem cells would be safer for me. I hope he's right because I'm following his lead. If the results don't concern him then I'm not going to worry about the results either. The chances are 50% that I would have infections within the first 100 days.

Easter Sunday 2003. I wake up early in the morning with the chills and a fever. I need to wrap a blanket around me when I walked into the kitchen because the chills were so bad. This is not good that I am drinking a lot of fluid early in the morning, which I don't normally do. I didn't sleep well last night because of the fever and chills.

The first thing I did this morning was to take my temperature, 101 degrees. I don't want to go to the hospital again- it is so demoralizing each time I get re-admitted. You take one step forward and two steps back.

The only good thing about going into the hospital on a holiday is that getting admitted is relatively quick in comparison to a normal day. We have to go through the whole routine of checking in, reviewing my medical history and the meds I'm taking, yada, yada, yada. I've already been admitted several times, but they need to get my medical history every time, so it still takes two hours to check in.
I'm able to lie on a gurney for most of the time. My back is really sore. What a way to spend Easter Sunday.

I can't walk out in the hall like I normally would because I'm quarantined in my room and hooked up to two separate IV lines. So I adlib exercising, standing next to my bed I started walking back and forth in place. I know its lame but that's all I can do for now.
Because I'm doing better overall Dr. Lowe doesn't feel the need to call in an infectious disease doctor for a consult. The pulmonologist comes in today and says he wants to continue the frequency of the C-pap procedures. I don't think he wants to hear what I think, so we'll just move on. I try to eat food that my family brings me as much as I can. I think I'm getting my taste buds back and my appetite.

A couple of days later I'm not hooked up to as many IV's so I can walk around the hospital more. I'm not willing to walk outside yet as I am using a walker for support, so for now I'm just going to wear a path in the hospital halls. Julie is going to stay with me Friday evening. The visitors' lounge is right down the hall and you can put together a makeshift bed, but I think she's getting one of the small beds that they can put in my room for her to sleep on overnight. I usually take my pills at night with graham crackers or saltine crackers and skim milk, so I don't get the bad taste residue from the pills and it seems to do the trick.

April 22, 2003. Dr. Lowe has been bringing this idea up for the past few days but I didn't want to think about it. I was hoping to avoid the procedure but no such luck. He proposed performing a bronchoscopy, which is used to find infectious organisms in the lungs, to find out if there is an infection, and to show what is not in the lungs. A tube is put down my throat into the lungs, which has a camera inside. The tube is placed down each lobe to look around, suction if needed or get a tissue sample. It would require me first being sedated through my IV. I'm glad I'd be sedated.

I'd be given a spray swab that numbs the back of my throat so the tube will go down easier. There could be some bleeding after the procedure due to the tissue sample taken, so I shouldn't panic. The bleeding may appear in my sputum. It takes a couple of days to get the results. The doctor on call wants blood cultures along with urine samples taken tonight, along with a chest x-ray taken tomorrow. I'm bracing for a terrible night of sleep.

April 26, 2003. The nurse comes in to do the normal morning blood draw from my picc line. The problem is the nurse can't initially get any blood to draw through the line, so Julie held my left arm in the air at 90 degrees and then it worked, so we need to pass that information onto others if that problem arises again.

April 27, 2003. I finally get outside to go walking in the afternoon with my brother Tomas. We sat outside by the entry way where everybody eats their lunch on nice days. I know I'll be tired at the end of the day from walking and sitting outside, that's the general idea. There's a check list of items we need to take along whenever I go outside: the wheelchair, my walker, a spit cup, a pillow for my back and a sheet in case I get cold.

April 28, 2003. My protein levels are down, Great! The antibiotics are working. I need to be on them for another week. The swelling and neuropathy (loss of feeling) in my feet are a result of the meds I'm on. The way to combat the swelling is to walk as much as I can, so that's what we're trying to do.

Rebecca, my nurse, is giving me a gammoglobulin infusion in my picc line today, which helps boost my immune system to help my body fight off pneumonia. The sputum cultures are normal from Monday. I guess normal is better than abnormal.

I don't need any more problems. I think I'm experiencing a morning hangover from all the meds I'm on. It's affecting my appetite and I cannot get discharged unless I show them that I have a good appetite and am eating everything on my food tray. Dr. Lowe says he's looking to send me home in a couple days (this means four days) without the picc line and oral antibiotics.

April 30, 2003. Peggy stops in this morning with a morning paper as I'm just getting ready to eat breakfast. Any one of my sisters stops in to check up on me before they go to work every day. That's cool; I like it when they stop by. For breakfast today, I'm eating the not so bad tasting pancakes with orange juice and milk. It's one of the better breakfasts I've recently ate. Dr. Lowe shows up and explains the antibiotic I'll be on now when I go home. It will be a shot given in my belly. My Dad will give it since he does it better than anybody else. I'll be going home on oxygen and the C-pap. I only need to use the oxygen when I'm walking, not when I'm sitting or lying down.

The nurses were going to put in a new picc line today. I know that Dr. Lowe wishes I didn't have a picc line in at all because of his fear of me getting another infection from the picc line site. Bu how would they be able to give me my infusions at home if I didn't have a line in?

I walked on the third floor with Trish, but for whatever reason, I have my oxygen all the way up to 6 liters, and I don't know what's up with my breathing. The infusions I get at the clinic are for the treatment of the myeloma but they can also suppress the immune system.

Dr. Lowe is consulting with the infectious disease doctor to see what his thoughts are on my treatment at this time, to make sure they are on the same page. My niece, Rachel, is staying with me for the rest of the morning and early afternoon. I've been sitting in the recliner in my room more than I had been before. It gets me out of bed, so when the nurse comes to change my bedding, I'm already out of the way, and I can sit closer to the window and get some vitamin D from the sun. It's also warmer by the window than it is anywhere else in the room.

My Mum comes to sit with me in the afternoon. She ran into one of my pulmonary doctors in the hallway and he says there is no change in my latest chest x-ray. One of my fingers has an infection by the corner of the fingernail and my Mum is changing the bandage today. The infectious disease doctor recommended that she should just cover it with gauze after putting Bacitracin on it. Rachel made me a root beer float today. It really tasted good. I'm getting my taste buds back after getting off of chemo.

My nurse for the day, Rebecca, listens to my lungs and they sound better. My oxygen level is up to four liters wearing the oxygen line at night. I've been down to two liters before so I guess my lungs aren't as healthy as I think they are. I have the c-pap put on between ten and eleven at night and leave it on until seven or eight in the morning. I usually don't wake up at all during the night while I'm wearing it, so I thank God for that.

I want out of this place! I hate this stinking mask I have to wear all night, I hate this daily regime I'm on all the time and I hate being around the hospital staff around the clock!

Alright, here we go, I'm getting discharged today! My family knows this process by heart. I get in the wheelchair and get wheeled down to front entrance of the hospital, whether I want to ride in the wheelchair or not. Peg and Rachel stay overnight at the farm and sleep in the living room next to my room. We know everything I need to have in my room before I go to bed. My Mum and Dad don't get to sleep until 11:45 pm. I think their worried about me getting a good night's sleep. Go to bed Mum and Dad, I'll be fine!

May 2, 2003. I ate a big breakfast today, my appetite is back. I have to put on a pair of those tight compression stockings. They help with keeping the circulation going in my lower legs and help prevent clots. It's just a pain to put them on every morning and take them off at night. I'll put them on myself, but a lot of times my Mum will help me especially after we wash them. I hate them but I need to wear them, so that's that.

I try to get out as much as I can to see family and visit them at home. They all live no more than twenty minutes away so it's not a long trip to any of their homes. I haven't driven myself anywhere for about a year. I don't think it would be too smart in my condition, plus I don't think my family would give me the keys to my car and I don't want to argue about it with all of them, I'd lose the argument. I don't really miss the driving that much anyway. They all know how to give me an infusion in the evening so I don't have to hurry home just for that. We can do the infusion at their house if we want and we have all the medical supplies.

May 10, 2003. I'm over at Mary's house and she and Julie are going to be doing the infusion this afternoon. They put the needle into the line and you can tell when it's working right, because the solution will start to slowly drip and it'll take the same amount every infusion (about 20 minutes) for the process to finish. I don't know what happened this time, but there was blood coming out of the picc line. That's not good, not good at all. So we called Dr. Lowe's office and he wanted us to go into the ER to get the line flushed out with heparin. It took longer to get into a room than it did for a nurse to do the procedure. They both felt bad but it was just a miscue. It could happen to anybody, its yesterday's news now. We move on.

May 11, 2003. Today it's Mothers Day! I'm tired but happy to be able to make my Mum's day enjoyable. She enjoys the day when everyone shows up with cards and flowers for her.

My back has been bothering me for over a year now but it's the least of my concerns. I can't do anything about it now. It will have to wait until I can have the stem cell transplant. So I either take the low dose morphine or I don't and deal with the discomfort. I get some good news, the picc line is coming out and my numbers from my most recent labs are the best that they have ever been.

Chapter Seventeen

Failing the Test

Dr. Lowe had a discussion with me and some family members about the stem cell transplant. He indicated that he felt I was making enough progress in the right direction to prepare for the procedures involved. He explained that I'm going to have the transplant at another hospital in the same city, which specializes in this type of transplant and has the equipment and staff to handle the entire procedure. The recovery period for a transplant is anywhere from a month to a year He indicated that a transplant coordinator would schedule my pulmonary function tests in the not too distant future, depending on how my lungs are recovering from the infections. I'm hoping my lungs are getting better every day but the test results will show the real truth.

It's the same routine of late. I go in for chest x-rays, and get the results a few days later. I've received some good news. The x-rays showed my lungs are getting better and the MRI showed my back has not changed at all, which means either the cancer has slowed down or the Zomata is helping. I walk as much as I can around the house since I have to be hooked up to oxygen when I walk. Dr. Lowe wants me to drop the oxygen down to two liters. We'll see how that goes. I guess if I'm gasping for air then it's time to crank the oxygen back up.

I know who the doctor is that will be performing the transplant, so I work on getting an appointment to see him. I'm still doing the nebulizer treatments four times a day along with using the flutter and the spirometer. I don't have to wear the c-pap every day now. It's every other day now for the first time in over a year that I haven't had to wear it every day.

I have to pass a series of breathing tests to be eligible for the transplant. I need to reach a minimum of 51 percent to pass the tests. I don't know how but I'll give it my best.

The test results came back a few days later and I failed the test. I had only reached 41 percent. So what do I do now? The only thing I could do was keep working on exercising my lungs with the breathing exercises. Dr. Lowe wasn't going to schedule another test for six months, so a stem cell transplant wasn't going to happen for at least that long. That's great, that's just great, more waiting but what else could I do, nothing! I move on and hope that I don't get some stupid infections in the meantime.

Since I have to wait for the six months to go by before another pulmonary function test can be done, I wanted to see as many qualified local spinal surgeons as possible that would examine me, look at my back x-rays and provide some options for addressing the compression fractures in my back. I realized that something could not be done immediately but I didn't want to waste any time in determining what my next steps would be in alleviating my back pain.

Chapter Eighteen

My Spine Findings

June 2, 2003. -I'm going to an appointment today to meet two spine doctors, that had reviewed my back x-rays, to discuss options and provide us some time to ask a lot of questions. I hope the results are good. I could use some good news about my back.

They did an evaluation to see if there was any spinal cord damage and found no damage. Great! The x-rays showed the spinal canal looks good and open. When vertebrae press on the spinal cord then that's when you have trouble. The x-rays and the MRI showed there is no spinal cord compression. The films did show the areas of concern. The back is separated into three areas 1) Cervical (C) - the neck area, 2) Thoracic (T) -middle part of the back, and 3) Lumbar (L) -lower back. That's how I remember it anyways.

I have compression fractures in C3, C4, T3, T4, T6, L4 and L5. I know that's sounds bad but now you know why my back hurts so much all the time. The compression fractures are a result of the vertebrae becoming weak and fracturing, putting a strain on the other vertebrae and causing other fractures. This is one of the results of having the multiple myeloma. It zaps the strength from the bones and the spine. All the coughing I've done over the months and the compression fractures created a lot of stress on my sternum, which ended up collapsing. My head is sitting lower over my chest rather than resting above my shoulders. My spine has the look of a hunchback. The whole problem causes a lot of discomfort when I stand for too long at any one time.

To me, pain is when it feels so bad that you need the pain pills. I'm not to that point yet, which is weird since I have so many fractures. But I know that I have a high tolerance for pain, which was evident when I played football in high school and college.

I am experiencing serious discomfort though, which I can live with for now since I have bigger fish to fry. Pain would be the deciding factor if and when something would be done for my back. I knew nothing was going to be done anyway until I had my transplant, but I needed to be thinking about future things as well. That is funny when you think about it coming from a person that has almost died a couple of times. The two doctors said they would not attempt anything to fix my back issues but did give some doctor names that I could consult with in the network.

The problem with me taking steroids for the myeloma is that they can cause the bone to deteriorate because they interfere with calcium absorption. So taking steroids on a daily basis for the myeloma is helping me with the cancer but is contributing to damage of my bones.

In order for me to get approval for any spinal surgery, I was going to need a surgeon who would take the chance to the do this type of procedure in the first place. This would entail scheduling appointments with the top spinal surgeons locally, and in the region. The aggravating thing is getting in to see the surgeons, who would be qualified. The time frame is anywhere from a month to several to get an appointment. The bad part about getting the appointment is the waiting and wondering. I was going crazy, well I wouldn't say crazy, but I was anxious to say the least, leading up to the day of the appointment.

I took all my x-rays with me and when the day came to go to my appointment, I must have had four or five of my siblings along. Picture one of those exam rooms cramped with two parents, four or five siblings, a doctor, myself and a nurse. It was pretty crowded but I didn't mind. I just wanted to hear what the surgeon had to say. All I wanted to hear was "YES I CAN HELP YOU"! I'm pretty good at reading doctors reactions so I can tell even before they open their mouth what the bottom line is.

The first doctor I saw gave all the reasons why he wouldn't attempt the surgery. The most dangerous reason was it was too high up in my spine and he wouldn't feel comfortable putting me at that much risk. I remember he asked me if I take pain pills, like that's the answer for what I need. I needed a surgeon who'd take the chance on me. The worse part of that appointment was seeing my family having to sit there and listen to the doctor tell me "NO" and why. The second surgeon I went to see in the insurance network was recommended by the first. His opinion was basically the same as the first surgeon. The surgery was too detailed and dangerous in my case and he wouldn't take the chance. I went to all this hassle to hear the response "NO" again. I wasn't surprised or really disappointed even. I didn't have a choice about what doctors I could see, or so I thought. My insurance would only cover certain surgeons in the health care network, so I had to jump through these hoops like everybody else to get something done.

In the back of my mind I had a feeling something was going to happen for the better. I even tried to get into the Mayo Clinic to see a surgeon who specialized in cases like mine. The waiting list was at least several months. Did I want to wait until that appointment? No, I wasn't going to wait that long.

Chapter Nineteen

Advocacy

I did not realize it at the time but my Mum and sisters Julie, Mary, and Trisha were working behind the scenes in researching additional options for me to help correct my back problems. They just returned from attending a large conference called the Multiple Myeloma Patient and Family Seminar in a hotel up near the Twin Cities, and they told me all about it. They said the "myeloma guru" from the Cedar Sinai Comprehensive Cancer Center spoke about new information researchers had found, results of various treatment options, and what the future holds for a cure.

There was also a panel of speakers that included Wisconsin's Multiple Myeloma Support Group founder and a gentleman who had had a procedure called Kyphoplasty- a procedure with perhaps the possibility to alleviate the back pain I have been experiencing for the past two years. This gentleman was an attorney from the Cleveland area who had had multiple myeloma. After having the Kyphoplasty procedure, he went from barely being able to tie his shoes to back on the golf course enjoying his favorite game.

In true Mary style, ever the opportunist on my behalf, she learned over to the other family members and said "We need to talk with that guy". And they did. When the panel was finished they all walked up to the stage, greeted their favorite MM Support Group leader with a hug, and approached the attorney with a pile of questions about the procedure, the recovery time, pain level before and after, and where do we go from here.

The attorney invited the family to join him for lunch and told the four of them that he'd had the Kyphoplasty procedure after he'd hurt his back. When it was identified that he had compression fractures, the doctors did a bone biopsy and he was diagnosed with multiple myeloma. Compression fractures are when the vertebrae have collapsed on the spine and one vertebra is sitting directly on top of the next vertebrae and the nerves in the spine. Kyphoplasty is the process of spreading the two vertebrae apart and putting something like "cement" in between them, which hardens and alleviates the nerve pain.

As they all talked, the lawyer revealed that he is golfing buddies with a doctor who is one of the inventors of the procedure. He explained the timeline and how everything worked, recovery, etc. The one question he couldn't answer was would this work for me? My family shared some of my story with him and could hardly eat; they were so excited to be talking with someone who had benefitted from the procedure.

After lunch was over, they didn't want to break their connection with him, and he must have sensed that they were a tough group, who didn't feel as if they had squeezed everything out of him yet, so what did he do? He pulled out his cell phone and called his doctor! What? We've been struggling and struggling with insurance companies, doctors, and each other and this guy just called the doctor, one of the inventers of the Kyphoplasty procedure, on his cell phone! Sometimes it's not what you know, it's who you know. The doctor answered his phone and said he was out in San Francisco speaking at a conference, but he offered up some physicians he'd trained in the Kyphoplasty procedure. Some of them my family had heard of before, others they hadn't. This doctor, Dr. Man who also was a surgeon, suggested that we call the orthopedic department at the clinic where he worked and schedule an appointment, and bring with us all the x-rays relating to my back issues.

The name of one of the local surgeons from my area came up in the conversation, and the doctor yelled into the phone "Why the hell couldn't he do anything? He trained under me!" And like only my sister Mary could respond she said "He's only done five of these procedures and didn't feel comfortable doing it, so we didn't want him." The lawyer asked Dr. Man if there was any way he could get me in for an appointment, and Dr. Man said he'd see what he could do. He explained over the phone that he'd done 12 of these surgeries in cases similar to mine on myeloma patients.

Another connection my family had made at the seminar was the representative from the company that produces the "cement" used for Kyphoplasty. They contacted him and he gave them the name of a doctor in Milwaukee that had done a number of these procedures successfully. They contacted him immediately to schedule an appointment.

When they got back from their trip, they were asking a lot of questions and made a connection with a doctor who could possibly help me down the road. You can definitely say this trip was a big success on my behalf. The Kyphoplasty procedures were going to be a short- term solution to a much bigger problem with my back, and I'm going to need consults for a much more invasive procedure.

They knew that this doctor was outside of my healthcare network and contacted my insurance company. The insurance company immediately declined covering my appointment with the Milwaukee doctor. My sisters would not take "NO" for an answer.

They went up the chain of command with the insurance company and got to a certain point and met a dead end. Either Julie or Mary read an article in a local magazine about a certification program offered at the University of Wisconsin for Patient Advocacy. Mary contacted the director of the program, Marnie, who also had cancer and was in remission.

She is an attorney and had to navigate through the healthcare system to get the treatments and doctors she wanted and felt there was a need to pass on everything she learned to law students that could use the information to assist future clients. When Mary met Marnie they hit it off right away. Mary had a gift for creating positive relationships with people and using those relationships to move her causes forward. Mary explained my situation with Marnie and took all the documentation she had to backup her information. Marnie had quite a few contacts at my insurance company and she contacted them about my case and the next thing I knew the company was going to cover my appointment. I can only imagine that the appointment would have cost hundreds of dollars, since it was with a specialist.

Dr. Rajib was the doctor in Milwaukee that I had my appointment with. After reviewing my skeletal x-rays, he felt that Kyphoplasty would provide me with a lot of relief and he would be willing to take my case. I got a big smile on my face and I would have jumped up and down if I had been able to. He was the first doctor that had given me some hope about my back. Now I felt like I had a longer range plan than before coming to the appointment. My sisters were elated to know that all their digging had paid off and I could get some pain relief for my back. One more roadblock was knocked over.

Now came the task of getting the actual Kyphoplasty procedure approved by the insurance company. Dr. Rajib submitted an authorization request to the insurance company to complete the procedure and was declined immediately, because he was out of network.

He submitted another authorization request to the insurance company, which provided more detail about my case, the benefits of the procedure, and indicated that there were no other doctors in my healthcare network that were able to complete the procedure. The second authorization came back declined as well.

Mary contacted Marnie again and filled her in on the outcome of the appointment and explained that there were not any doctors in the network that would attempt the procedure and provided all the benefits I would realize from having the procedure. Marnie said she wanted to speak with me about the procedure, so she gave me a call and we talked about the entire journey we had taken in finding Dr. Rajib and learning about Kyphoplasty. I think our discussion, in conjunction with her discussion with Mary, made all the difference in her going to bat for me. Marnie happened to know the president of my insurance company and contacted him about my case. She advocated for me to have the procedure and the next thing I knew the insurance company approved me to have the procedure. Thank goodness for my family, Marnie, and Dr. Rajib. There seems like there is some light at the end of the tunnel. Now I need to get through the stem cell transplant, which won't be a small undertaking, to take advantage of completing this procedure.

Chapter Twenty

Roadblocks

June 30, 2003. I went to my regularly scheduled appointment with my parents to get my blood work done and to meet with Dr. Lowe for an exam. The highlight of this appointment is my doctor telling us that I am in REMISSION. It's a little over one year since I was diagnosed. My parents were very happy to hear the news. I thought I'd be more excited but I didn't get as excited as I thought I would, maybe because I've seen my health change in an instant. My Mum called all my sisters to give them the news. They screamed for joy and were doing the happy dance. My brothers showed less excitement, but that's my brothers for you. They are more cautious in displaying their emotions. I started to get a slight cough and the chills early Monday evening. My temperature was elevated to 101 degrees. I took 500 milligrams of Tylenol and my temperature dropped to 101.9. I took another Tylenol at 10:00pm.

July 1, 2003. I woke up at 6:00am and took my temp because my forehead felt hot and the thermometer read 101.8. Just to be safe, I went in to Dr. Lowe's office for an exam and consult about the change in condition. He took my temp and it was 101.3. My oxygen level (Pulse Ox) was 89%. I should have readings in the high 90's. Dr. Lowe says this is a chronic change and I'm being admitted to the hospital again. My countdown to a transplant is dealt another setback. I am readmitted to the hospital for what seems like the tenth time and taken to Six East. Since I have been on this floor so many times I should get my choice of what room I am assigned.

Dr. Lowe diagnosed the problem as a reoccurrence of the pneumonia. I was put back on antibiotics. Respiratory therapy is in shortly thereafter for a nebulizer and a back vibrator session. I also have labs done.

I'm exhausted from no rest the previous night, which I didn't tell anybody. I knew these symptoms were going to take me back to the hospital. The thermometer is reading 100 degrees early in the afternoon. As evening approached, the temp started to elevate to 102 degrees, which usually is the case. I took two Tylenol and the temp dropped somewhat before my Mum left at 9:00pm.

The next ten days I was doing everything I could to exercise my lungs along with taking the antibiotics. I had the nebulizer treatments four times a day. I used the spirometer machine every hour. The back vibrator I did twice a day.

My cousin Danny, who lives out in California, came to visit me. He wanted me to meet his girlfriend and visit with her. It seems she was recently diagnosed with breast cancer and he felt I could give her some advice on dealing with it. I don't know what I could say to help out a breast cancer patient. It is a whole different story than my case but if she wants to talk I'd be a good listener. He said she had a tumor already removed and she'd be starting the chemotherapy very soon. He described to me a picture of what was going on in her case so I knew something about it when we talked. We have a nice conversation and she asked a couple of questions about my treatment. The only thing I commented on to her was the chemotherapy was going to be tough on her body, but its' tough on everybody's, so that's its job. I told her she'll get through it and wished her luck.

I will be unable to take the pulmonary function test, which is the determining factor in going ahead with the stem cell transplant, because of my continuing lung issues. My patience is starting to wear thin.

My brother Steve, who lives in Portland, Oregon came back home to visit. The last time I saw him was nine months ago. I am sure he was surprised at my appearance. My hair had fallen out from the chemo drugs, I had lost a bit of weight and height, and I was wearing my brace which helped to hold my head up. Steve had made the comment when he went home last time that my health would be different the next time we would see each other. I'd either be in isolation following my transplant or I'd be at home waiting for the transplant to proceed. My health changes on a daily basis.

Dr. Lowe has a meeting with my parents and explains that due to my lung problems that reappeared, the transplant is postponed. I'm not surprised; the writing was on the wall. The pneumonia saw to that. If I was to have the transplant now it would be life threatening to go ahead with it. I have enough problems now to know I didn't need to add more. The only way to get my lungs to recover is to exercise them and take more time to let them heal. Antibiotics will only do so much for you. I was going to be getting a couple of antibiotics sent home with me to help in recovering from the pneumonia. I hope one thing that people learn while reading this book is to take care of their lungs and not to take their health for granted.

July 3, 2003. I'm moving from room 663 to room 669 just around the corner, facing the south side of the hospital, with a window view of the busy street right next to the hospital and the lake. The room is bigger so I lucked out with the view and more room.

I couldn't sleep on a normal hospital mattress because my back was so sore all the time. The nursing staff put a foam mat, the size of the bed, over the mattress and it worked out perfect. God love that nurse who came up with that idea and found that mat. When I moved to the new room we took the foam mat too.

Chapter Twenty One

Fireworks on the Roof

July 4, 2003. The typical morning schedule for me was breakfast at 7:15am, the C-pap was removed shortly after, and then a nurse would come in to get my vitals (blood pressure, temperature, pulse). The highlight for me was the nurse asking me my number on the pain scale from 1 to 10. I said today was a three; normally I'd say my pain level was between three and six. I never said I had a ten on the pain scale, which would have probably had me moaning if the pain was that bad. My temperature was 99 degrees this morning; it was as high as 102 degrees during the night. When it's that high, it is too uncomfortable to try and sleep.

My breakfast arrived at 7:30. I try to eat the same foods I normally would eat at home for breakfast. Breakfast was the highlight of my day for hospital food. I had two small packets of cereal with skim milk, toast with jelly, and some grapes.

My Mum and Dad showed up at 9:15 to visit. I always liked it when my parents came to sit with me. My Mum would always check the room to make sure everything was where it should be and up to her standards as soon as she arrived. My Dad would usually ask me "how'd I sleep" and how I felt in the morning, things like that, and then he'd sit down to read the morning paper if I had it or if I didn't he'd read one of his paperback books of western stories he brought along from home. They had to put on the gowns and masks like everyone else, unfortunately. It didn't bother my Mum as much, but my Dad didn't like putting the gown and mask on. It makes your body temperature rise and the mask makes your breathing labored.

My Dad has COPD, so anything that affects his breathing is bothersome to him. My breathing is really labored on this day so we turned my oxygen up to four liters from the two that I was on.

111

It's 10:15am and my temperature has spiked back up to 102 degrees. I took a Tylenol and it helped a little bit. Today's a rough day though. My temperature has been up all day, so I feel lousy and I don't have an appetite. I need to keep my strength up taking in calories but I wasn't hungry today. It is sunny outside and the temperature is warm and I'm stuck in this place on a nice day. It sucks!

Since my sputum is still being collected and analyzed, the infectious disease doctor came in to check on my condition. After a short talk to ask how I'd been feeling the past few days he indicated that they are trying to determine if what is going on in my lungs is bacterial or fungal. He indicates that I have a yeast infection and prescribes an antibiotic, Caspofungin.

I've been getting three nebulizer treatments a day, but now with this latest breathing issue, my doctor increases the treatments to six a day. I didn't mind the nebulizer treatments as I always felt some relief from them. All you do is take in deep breaths of the mist Albuterol through a tube, and it goes down your throat into the lungs and then you breathe it out. The Albuterol is supposed to open up the bronchial tubes in the lungs and help make breathing easier. I have a lot of crackling in my lungs. It's more noticeable when I'm sleeping.

The pulmonary doctor comes in at 12:30 to ask me some questions and go over what he saw on my chest x-ray I had earlier this morning. The doctor listens to my lungs and says that the base in my right lung looks worse than a couple of days ago. I wasn't making enough antibodies, which is a characteristic of myeloma. The solution is to introduce an immunoglobulin into my treatment regime to fight off infections.

Along with the nebulizer treatments for my lungs, the nurses gave me a device called a "flutter" which is like a whistle you blow into. It is suppose to help in moving the mucous out of the lungs. I could tell that the staff was pulling out all the stops in finding additional therapies for my lungs.

One pulmonologist says one thing and the infectious disease doctor says another; who do you believe at this point? Their recommendation could obviously alter Dr. Lowe's course of treatment. Whose diagnosis and recommendation of treatment do you go with? I'm glad my Dr. Lowe has to make that call with input.

I wasn't feeling great about being in the hospital on the Fourth of July. This was the second year in a row that I was spending it in the hospital. My brother Tomas came up with the brainy idea that we should go up to the top of the parking garage and watch the fireworks. I don't know if we'd be able to see the fireworks. We weren't the only ones to have this idea because when he wheeled me out on the east side of the parking ramp a dozen other patients and family members were standing up waiting to see the fireworks as well. It was a great view of the capital building all lit up and it was a warm night with a slight breeze. I have to admit it was a lot better than sitting in the room watching it on the tube. I couldn't believe how great a view we had and we could see every fireworks display going off on the cities' north side. The best part of it was that after the half hour show we didn't have to fight traffic. I just sat down in the wheelchair and Tomas wheeled me back to the service elevator and we went back to the room. No traffic jams, Cool!

July 5, 2003. One of my sisters would always show up early in the morning before they went to work. They would stop by to see how I was feeling and bring me something to read that day, such as the newspaper or a sports magazine. Then they would call my Mum and give her a morning update on how I am and what my schedule was going to be for the day.

Since they all worked and would not be at the hospital during the day, Mum and Dad would take turns coming to sit with me. I looked forward to that part of the day. We'd talk about what tests Dr. Lowe had ordered and when he was going to stop by for his daily rounds. It's a routine you come to expect.

The tingling neuropathy in my fingers and feet, which is caused by the medications, is about the same. The numbness is worse in my feet and ankles. I hardly have any feeling but that's to be expected. Some patients can decide to reduce the dosage of thalidomide they take because of the neuropathy. The hell with it, let's keep going with the same milligrams, it's not that big a deal to me. Walking is supposed to help but it's not helping in my case. I've tried acupuncture and electric stimulation. They work to a point but when I'm on this high a dosage, I question how much good both of those do for the neuropathy.

It's a little after six o'clock at night and I just finished eating and Julie stops by to visit. I like to go for a walk after dinner to help me sleep better at night. My family would usually stay past the normal 8 o'clock deadline for family or visitors to leave the hospital. The nurse didn't seem to mind too much, I was glad to have the company when everything was quiet at night. When it's quiet I have too much time to think about all the things that could go wrong.

July 7, 2003. Dr. Lowe requested they take cultures from my nose, fingers and eyes for MRSA. If the cultures come back positive I wouldn't be able to walk out in the halls. I would have to walk in place in my room to get some exercise and not go stir crazy being in this room all day. It's not good in my case to be in bed all day. I have a history of developing blood clots in my legs, so that's another reason I need to get up and move around.

The number of different doctors who would come in to check up on my condition would change from day to day. I had two oncology doctors, four pulmonary doctors, and one infectious disease doctor. I usually find out the day before who is going to be stopping in and what tests they have requested. The chest x-rays and MRI's are always a long, drawn- out process.

July 8, 2003. I was finally taken off the electorcardiam (EKG) the nurses used to measure my body's core numbers. The nebulizer treatments are working, my lungs are sounding better, and there is not as much crackling when the doctor's listens to me taking deep breaths.

One of the nurses, Monica, doesn't like a messy room and she lets me know it by saying so to me. Dr. Lowe decides that when I get my Zomata treatments once a month that I'll also be getting an immunoglobulin treatment as well. This should increase my antibodies and help fight off infections.

My Dad came by to sit and go for a walk with me in the halls. My Dad could walk all day with me. I always walked more when I'm with him. I think it's a guy thing. I'm still coughing up some slugs but I'm feeling better. The hospital rents out VCRs and we rented the movie "The Three Kings", which was pretty good.

July 10, 2003. I'm still wearing the c-pap at night, I hate it but that's what we have to do. I'm getting tired of the staff, seeing the same people day after day, and they're getting tired of me too, I can tell. The pulmonologist says my chest x-ray looks good and he thinks I'm well enough to be discharged. So I'm hopeful but we'll see. I've been through this too many times to get my hopes up for a quick discharge.

The home health people want to set up a time to go over instructions on giving me IV's at home that my sister or Dad could administer. My family has been trained on doing this before so they have a pretty good idea about how to start the process. The hardest part is getting the needle into the vein without the vein rolling, which happens a lot in my case, so it's tricky and you have to watch it or else the solution will fill up your arm and the area gets bloated. I know what it looks like. It happened before, and you've wasted all that solution you were going to use. I was hoping I'd be discharged today, but it wasn't meant to be. I guess it will be tomorrow so here comes another night in the hospital.

July 11, 2003. To my surprise I'm getting released today. I'm ready to go home since I'm good and tired of this place after ten days. My temp has dropped to 97.6. All the breathing exercises along with the antibiotics have worked to cure my pneumonia. Based on where my health is right now, my doctor feels it would be life-threatening to try and go ahead with a stem cell transplant at this point. My lungs are not healed where they need to be and my immune system is nowhere near where it should be, so.... we wait. Patience is a virtue. I like the sound of that. I was hoping to be in the hospital 2, 3, 5 days, tops, but it didn't work out that way.

I'll have to go back on the c-pap at night when I go to bed and I'm not looking forward to wearing that mask all night. I'm sure my Dad doesn't really want to put it back on me, but that's what the doctor wants, so we do it. He has a good handle on whether it's adjusted correctly. Dr. Lowe brought up a good point about having someone come and check the settings of the cpap machine I'll have at home to make sure it's operating correctly and the settings are right. It wouldn't make sense to go to all the trouble of getting it approved by my insurance to have it at home and wear it at night and then not get the full benefits of wearing it.

July 12, 2003. I slept through the night with the mask on. I was really tired from all the meds and the moving around to get back on my schedule at home. The home health nurse came today and examined my picc line and found some blood in it. She flushed it with saline and heparin and indicated that this is the procedure to follow if we find blood in the line again. The white valve is to remain open, which is how air probably got into the line and couldn't escape.

August 15, 2003. I have a doctor's appointment today- labs and a consult with Dr. Lowe, plus I finish with my Zomata (bone strengthening) infusion. My weight has jumped up to 189.2 pounds. I'll need every bit of that weight when I go in for the transplant, because I won't be eating much food then.

August 22, 2003. A week later, at a follow up doctor's appointment, my weight continues to rise- up to 193 pounds. My lab work looks good, my blood pressure is 120/80; my temperature is 97.1. Dr. Lowe orders a CT scan to look at my lungs, and the results look good. I don't have to be back to see Dr. Lowe for a month. Great news! In the meantime, I'm doing everything I can at home to be a hundred- percent for the stem cell transplant that's coming up in a couple of months.

August 31, 2003. We had scheduled an appointment with Dr. Man, who Mary, Julie, Trish and my Mum had heard about from the lawyer from Ohio. His clinic is eleven hours away, in Cleveland, Ohio at the Cleveland Clinic. We needed to plan ahead how we were going to travel there. I'm determined to at least meet this guy and see what he has to say once he looks at my x-rays and reads my medical history. I was able to get an appointment at the clinic's spinal surgeon's department a few months down the road, but, as it turns out the clinic had a cancellation and there was an opening for the coming Monday morning. There are no coincidences.

Today is Wednesday, so I don't know if I can make that appointment, but I'm going to try. I told the receptionist I'd call her back by the end of the day. I'd already checked on the prices to fly and it was too expensive to fly on such short notice, so we were going to drive to the clinic. I called Julie to see if she would be willing to make the trip with me, since I felt she had the best chance of being able to take off from work on short notice. I'm not physically strong enough to go by myself. Julie called back in an hour and said she'd go with me. I'm not surprised. Julie is like that, flexible and dependable. I can always ask her to help and she will. She had already checked out a rental car when she called me back and let me know we were set to go.

We may need a place to stay if we arrived earlier so I managed to locate a hotel right next to the clinic. The clinic has a shuttle bus that picks up patients from area hotels every 15 minutes along its route, and our hotel was one of the regular stops on its route, which is good since parking is near impossible close to the clinic. We left at 8 p.m. on Sunday night and drove the whole way there, arriving in Cleveland on Monday morning around 6:00 am.

The good thing about traveling at that time of the night is that we missed rush hour traffic going through Chicago. The closer we got to the clinic the more nervous I felt. I guess it was finding out about the unknown or possibly bad news.

I thought we were just going to freshen up someplace and get some breakfast and head over to the clinic, but Jules wanted to take a shower. I was like "what, you gotta be kidding; we're going to check into a hotel for a couple of hours?" I thought about it for a little bit and agreed. Jules, at the last minute decided to go on this trip with me, take off work, drive all night, and make it here on time. I wasn't going to argue at this point. So we checked in and I laid down for a couple of hours. Then I took a shower after Jules and we were good to go. She was right, we needed a shower to wake up and refresh ourselves. When we were ready we took the shuttle bus to the clinic, which worked out great. I couldn't believe we made it here after such short notice, but we did. Thanks Jules!

Chapter Twenty Two

Appointment Doesn't Go As Expected

September 5, 2003. The first thing I did when we arrived for the appointment was check in at the front desk. I gave the scheduling person my name and who I was there to see. She asked me who I was here to see and I told her again. She had me wait one minute while she checked on something. I was getting nervous something was going to go wrong with this conversation. She called me up to the front desk again and told me that Dr. Man was in surgery today and he'd be unable to see me. I was floored and so disappointed. I couldn't believe we drove all this way only to have Dr. Man be unable to see me. I don't understand why the scheduling person made this appointment if I wasn't going to see him. Now what? I hoped we didn't come all this way for nothing.

I presented my insurance card and received a questionnaire regarding my back pain. A financial counselor asked to see me. The counselor had never heard of my insurance coverage. I wasn't surprised since we lived 11 hours away from here in another state. We explained to the counselor that my insurance company is a major health insurance corporation in the area we live in.

She tried to call the insurance company and there was no answer (due to the one hour time difference). We asked how much the appointment would cost for today. She indicated the normal cost is $650.00 and they take major credit cards. She would charge $250.00 for now and process the claim through my insurance carrier. If the claim was denied, I'd be responsible for the difference. So, if I wanted to see a doctor for a consult it'll cost $250.00 to do that. We didn't come all this way for nothing so I pulled out the plastic. Luckily, I was going to see a couple of the surgeon's colleagues. These weren't the people I wanted to see but it's the next best thing. They called my name after about forty-five minutes of waiting and led us into an exam room, where we waited and waited and waited. My back was bothering me sitting in the chair they had in the exam room. I laid down on the exam table for a little relief and it helped.

When the first person came in he introduced himself as an intern who was doing a fellowship at the clinic and he'd be taking down my background medical history for the surgeon. Then he said that a doctor would be in shortly. I could hear them speaking outside in the hallway, looking at my x-rays. I could hear every little negative thing they were saying about my case. Sitting there, I was praying that the doctor could give me some good news himself.

The intern came back in with the doctor. The doctor had the title of Fellow Spine Specialist. This specialist reviews patient's medical history and consults with the surgeon I'm hoping to see. This was the first time the intern and specialist had seen the films I brought with me. The intern indicated that my spine had severe kyphosis in T1 and T2 which are compressed, T9 is minimal, and osteoporosis is in T7 and T8 area. Kyphosis is severe rounding of the upper spine. The intern said that surgery would be too dangerous in the area of my cervical spine. The second doctor's assessment was there is severe angulation (obstructive bend) in my cervical and upper thoracic spine. With multiple myeloma, a risk factor or concern is the degree of bone loss and risk with fixation devices. The fusion –type surgery would involve posture correction and fusion of the spine.

The risks of spinal fusion in my case were several. 1) The screws could loosen 2) the thinning of the bone in the event the disease returns 3) the chance of spinal cord injuries-as the surgeons are in there moving the spinal cord 4) the possibility of nerve injury with the surgeons working around the nerves.

The specialist made a recommendation for a less evasive option being a kyphosis orthotics apparatus which would help my posture somewhat but the degree of kyphosis in this case is severe and he wasn't sure of the benefits. That assessment didn't sound good at all but this is what I drove here for. Again all this talk is speculation at this meeting because these doctors aren't surgeons. I needed to talk with the surgeon. This was my last hope as of right now and what they are saying doesn't sound good. This meeting wasn't going anywhere with the doctors making unsure recommendations.

The only hope that I have is that the specialist said they have my records and that Dr. Man should see me in person and review my case. They put a note in my file to "see so and so specifically". That was all I had to hold out hope for now. So I have no other choice but to agree. We set up another appointment and proceeded to head back home.

We left the appointment after about an hour. I am disappointed that we don't get to see Dr. Man but it is short notice and we'd have to see these doctors for a consult anyway before I could see him. We have to start somewhere with this and they recommended that I see Dr. Man, which is what I was trying to do to begin with. We are taking small steps, but we are moving forward.

We have packed our bags in the morning before we left the hotel so we started driving home after the appointment. I wouldn't say the consult was a success but it wasn't a failure either, so I have some glimmer of hope. The weather was nice driving back home today. The sun was out and that is good to see because the trip just dragged on driving back home. My next appointment would be with Dr. Man. We knew where we were at in the process now.

The trip down here was a long drive but driving back home was going to be even longer. Returning trips are always longer aren't they?

We had been on the road for over ten hours when we came into downtown Chicago at rush hour. We slowed to a crawl. I knew we might run into this slowdown at this time of day so I wasn't going to worry about it, you can't let it get to you. Julie had other ideas. I guess being on the road for so long and putting up with the traffic jams drove her to display the perfect example of road rage. The amount of traffic wasn't good for Julie. I don't know if it was any one driver cutting her off that set her off but she got really upset. I think being in the car all day had a lot to do with it, because I can't remember the last time I saw Julie this upset. It wasn't doing any good. I was trying to settle her down but she just wanted to get through the traffic. (We'll probably laugh about it later) but for now I'm just trying to stop her from wrecking the car. It takes about an hour of stopping and starting to get through the city and we're three hours away from home. But we make it back safe. I promised myself that the next time we went back to see the surgeon that we'd fly rather than drive, if we could make it work financially. For Julie to drive down to the clinic on such short notice was a big help. I'm sure she's never going to let me forget that.

Chapter Twenty Three

Transplant Schedule

September 9, 2003. Today I have an appointment with Dr. Short, the transplant doctor. I'll be meeting with him in a different hospital than where I normally go. It takes a little time to find our way around once we get there. The layout of the hospital seems like a maze you need to get around in. The doctor asks about my pulmonary resting oxygen rate and the nurse checks it with the pulse-ox meter and it is ninety five. The doctor makes me walk around the modular and then rechecks my number. It's still ninety-four, so that is a big improvement. I have come a long way in 15 months and it seems like I have a long way to go yet. This is my marathon.

I tell Dr. Short that the numbness in my feet goes all the way up to my calves and that it's due to that the three hundred milligrams a day of thalidomide that Dr. Lowe prescribed. I catch a break when the transplant doctor says that if the pulmonary doctor from this hospital sees stability in my lungs, then I can get off the thalidomide prior to the transplant, which I'm hoping would mean that the numbness would go down considerably in my feet.

Dr. Short explains the transplant and stem cell process. I'll be taking higher doses of chemotherapy up to two weeks prior to the transplant, to clear up any residual myeloma cells. Then I will be in a quarantined wing of the hospital with other transplant patients. Dr. Short will reschedule his tests around my October appointment with the pulmonary doctor.

September 10, 2003. A month ago I saw a pulmonary function doctor to test my breathing when I was walking on a treadmill at program pace for twenty five to thirty minutes. I tested on three liters of oxygen at eighty-nine percent. Today when I completed the same test, my numbers are ninety four percent, so all the exercises I've been doing have definitely helped, and I'm sure the pulmonary doctor and Dr. Short will be happy to see these results. I'm ready for the transplant right now.

September 23, 2003. I have an appointment today with Dr. Lowe to see how I'm doing before the stem cell transplant. My weight has been steady at 192 pounds. My lungs sound good, even though there was some crackling in the bottom lobes, a gradual improvement though. Dr. Lowe is going to drop down the thalidomide from 300 milligrams to 200 milligrams. I hope the numbness will decrease somewhat from this change, but we'll see soon enough. Dr. Lowe cut my Remeron from 30 milligrams to 15 milligrams. The Remeron I take is an antidepressant Dr. Lowe prescribed.

I have been taking a medication called Decidron and the frequency and dosage have been reduced to once a month on 40 milligrams. The Decidron relieves inflammation in the body, specifically swelling or edema of tumors of the spine. I'm hoping all these med changes will help me sleep better and feel normal for a while anyway. I'm happy with the new list of dosages I'll be taking. At the end of the appointment, I stayed to get my Zomata treatment, the bone strengthening drug.

October 23, 2003. I have an appointment with Dr. Lowe today. He asks about a chest cold I've had for the last five days and says he wants to go back on the bi-pap every night and to have nebulizer treatments three times a day. My Mum asks Dr. Lowe questions about the notes she recorded from meeting with the pulmonologist recently.

I was on Remeron, which helps with memory, and now I'm going to be off of it for the foreseeable future. Why is that? The negative side effects I am experiencing are irritability and mood swings. I'm going to start taking a vitamin supplement of B12/B6, because vitamin introduction can assist with nerve dysfunction, which I'm having due to the thalidomide. I get to decide whichever I want to take. I'll take both B vitamins every day.

October 29, 2003. I have another appointment with my pulmonologist today. We review my daily activity of exercise and being on the bi-pap with oxygen. He thinks an echocardiogram will be a good test to see how the heart is working in conjunction with the lungs. He discusses the risks of a bone marrow transplant relating to my lung infections. He listens to my lungs and they sound pretty clear, just a few crackles on the left side. He wants to see me back in three to four months, which is after my transplant.

Later the same day I have an appointment with the transplant doctor, Dr. Short .He gives me a lung function test right away to measure my lung volume and differential capacity. He informs me that my echocardiogram test will be scheduled for November twentieth. I'll have my blood cells collected in three weeks. The stem cell transplant is set for the early part of January.

The chemotherapy drug I'll be taking at the time of the transplant is Cytoxin. The dosage will be large enough to cause my red blood cell count to drop very low. The hope is that the drug will kill the rapidly dividing cancer cells before the transplant, when I'm in the transplant wing of the hospital. The second chemotherapy drug I'll be taking is called Melphalan, which is a very strong drug. The combination of the Cytoxin and the Melphalan is called a chemotherapy "cocktail". It is not a cocktail I will enjoy.

Chapter Twenty Four

Another Ray of Hope

November 20, 2003. Today is the day I'm going to see an orthopedic surgeon about the possibility of having the Kyphoplasty procedure. The Kyphoplasty procedure fills in areas in the spine that are missing cartilage with the "cement" compound, which will help minimize the spine from pinching more of the nerves in my spine. The doctor I am going to be hopefully meeting with today performs 75% of the Kyphoplasty procedures in the state right now. So he has a lot of experience. I just hope he has enough experience for a case like mine. My lungs are finally well enough to see this doctor. He will be seeing me at a hospital in Milwaukee. My sisters Peggy and Mary brought along my most recent back x-rays to hopefully get in to see this guy. I was really nervous that he would see my x-rays and say "sorry, there's nothing I can do for you". I was dreading that he would say there is so much damage and he could not possibly attempt the procedure. To me, the message would be there is no hope and hope is all I have.

We were lucky enough to get in and see the doctor in between consults he had that day. I gave him a high level overview of where I have been and where I am going with my treatment plan. I nervously watched as he looked at my x-rays and explained to us what was going on in my spine at this moment. After giving me all this medical jargon I cut to the chase and asked him if he could help me. I could hardly breathe in anticipation of his response. His answer was—YES, he could help! I was so relieved and my sisters were overjoyed. The doctor said at most he'd only do the procedure on three vertebrae in one appointment.

The thoracic area, which was giving me the most discomfort, is where he'd start. The three in particular would be T4, T6 and T11. The surgery would be completed on an outpatient basis, so if everything went well I could go home the same day. Sweet! I'd need to get an updated back x-ray and since this doctor and hospital were out of my insurance network I would have to go back to my oncologist and ask him to assist in getting the x-ray taken. I didn't know if he would help with this or not since the procedure was going to be done at another hospital.

As our appointment was winding down the doctor made a point to say I should have come to him sooner. I'm thinking yeah, I would have if not for the repeated pneumonias, infections, and MRSA. One doctor is looking at one aspect of my case and a different doctor is looking at a different aspect. It was all about prioritizing what was the most important to address first, and obviously it was to save my life first and foremost.

Getting in to get an x-ray as soon as possible is not easy. There's usually a backlog of patients needing full spinal x-rays, so I was thinking it might be a few weeks before I could get in. I went ahead and made my appointment after Dr. Lowe put in the order for the x-ray and put my name on the will-call list in case someone cancels an appointment and you can get in sooner. It doesn't usually happen but sometimes you get lucky and someone cancels, which happened in my case. Unbelievable, I was able to get in only a week after I called to schedule the appointment. Now we had to wait and see if I could get this approved through my insurance and get it done before my stem cell transplant or if I'd have to wait until after. That decision would be out of my hands and a decision was up to the transplant doctor.

I realized going in to meet with Dr. Short, to discuss having the Kyphoplasty, that he wasn't going to be too keen on me moving ahead with my back so close to my transplant. I was juggling a lot at one time but my back was bothering me so bad I had to try and make it work.

My transplant doctor didn't care about my back pain; he was concerned with the transplant. The transplant was set up to get started the first week of the year so it was getting close. My transplant doctor nixed the idea of me trying to schedule a Kyphoplasty procedure before my transplant and said I would have to wait until after, since the transplant is what I had been working towards all along. Yeah, I was disappointed but what could I do, the decision was made and it was out of my hands. Un-beknownst to me the majority of my family thought I was too anxious in wanting to have the Kyphoplasty and felt that I had a small window of time to get the transplant done, since I had so many issues with my lungs and infections. They also felt that my priority should have been getting the transplant done first to deal with the cancer. I guess Dr. Short made the right call.

December 12, 2003. Today is testing day for me at the transplant hospital. I'm not nervous, I'm either going to pass or fail. I will be having blood work done, a CT scan, a bone marrow biopsy and pulmonary function test. I hope I will be able to pass all the tests or my transplant will be postponed again. My blood counts were just about perfect a week ago, but that was a week ago.

It wasn't the best day to go in for tests. Wednesday morning is the worst time to schedule appointments, according to another patient, because the doctors and nurses have a weekly staff meeting every Wednesday. Four lab technicians called in sick today so appointment times are going to back up more now. When it rains it pours.

When I was getting ready for the CT scan I had to drink two big paper cups of a dye, which shows up on the scan for the technicians to be able to see my insides more clearly. It doesn't taste very good so I had to force it down. I just chugged it the best I could. The scan itself takes about thirty minutes. I had an IV in my arm so it was kind of tricky to get this setup just right. I lay down on the table on my back and the machine would slide me far enough into the machine so that three quarters of my body is scanned. I close my eyes once they start the procedure. I don't get claustrophobic in being in restrictive small places, so I try to relax and hope there aren't any mistakes in taking the scans because my back is getting sore. The technician in charge keeps asking me how I'm doing. I lie and say I'm doing all right because I want to get this over with, and I have to lay still for the procedure. The last fifteen minutes of the test seemed like it took forever.

First the blood draw, then the CT scan and now the biopsy. This would be the worst procedure today. The biopsy itself isn't that big a deal if enough anesthesia is given ahead of time. Like I said, I've had them before so I know what to expect. I will be lying on my side with a pillow between my legs to help my back pain. Once the nurse gives me the shot I will fall asleep almost immediately. The doctor uses a T shaped instrument and screws it down into my hip bone. Once he gets to the right location he takes samples of my bone marrow, which will be used to determine the level of cancer cells in my pelvic area. The biopsy is taken there because doctors think it is a central point of the body and would give the best indicator of the cancer level in the marrow. I don't remember the procedure at all. It only took twenty minutes and I continued to sleep for an additional half hour, snoring like crazy. When I snore you know I'm sleeping soundly. Maybe I should take some of that anesthesia every night so I would get a good night's sleep.

It's been six months since my last pulmonary function test and hope I'll do ok. I need to score better than 50 % to pass the test to be cleared for the stem cell transplant. I don't want to fail again and have to wait another six months. I get in the "bubble" and the doctor directs me through the testing. I didn't feel too confident once we finished the testing. I hope I passed. I'd be really disappointed this time if I didn't. It takes a few days to get the results back and I was getting anxious. I cannot fail this again!

December 15, 2003. I don't believe it, I passed! I don't know how but I passed, and just like that we move on to getting me scheduled for the procedure. The transplant will take place the first week of next year. This was only a few weeks away. I needed to keep exercising, and do everything I can to get my health even better between now and then.

Chapter Twenty Five

Moving Forward

Dr. Lowe wanted to schedule an appointment for lab work. He was going to get the results and confer with my pulmonary doctor about the results. He explains there is a window open only for so long and still be aggressive with the myeloma treatment. Dr. Lowe was moving forward but still cautious. I guess you could call his decisions "cautiously aggressive". With my history of lung infections, I could see why he would have those reasons for stating that there's only a short window of opportunity for getting the transplant completed.

I am going to be using my own blood stem cells for the transplant. The doctor felt there is the best chance of success using my own. I'd be at the hospital for two appointments on consecutive days for a three hour period each time. The nurse would collect a certain amount of my cells each time in order to have enough for the entire process. The time it took might be longer the second day depending on how many cells the transplant doctor needed. It isn't a problem for me, I'm not feeling fatigued during or after the procedure either day. The blood is frozen until it is needed, which in my case would be a couple of months.

The second day is a little rockier than the first. The nurse happens to let the needle come out of my vein and we couldn't get the bleeding stopped, so a little bit of blood is leaking out of my arm. I'm not worried. It didn't gross me out when I saw it. I just wanted to get the procedure over with. My Mum, Dad, and sisters are in the room at one time or another while all this is going on. It's a lengthy and slow process. My body is doing all the work, and my family gives me a hand if I need something to eat or drink.

Alright, now that my cells have been collected we wait for the transplant date to arrive. In the meantime I am doing my routine, exercising, eating, and getting enough sleep. Dr. Short wants me to gain as much weight as I can because I'm not going to eat much after the transplant.

I don't believe it. I developed a severe cold, enough that I needed to go in for an x-ray of my lungs, the results which showed that I developed bronchitis. The transplant will be pushed back another couple of weeks. Oh well, I waited this long, what's another month? At least I don't have to take another pulmonary function test to be cleared for the transplant.

The type of transplant I'll be getting is called an autologous stem cell transplant. For this procedure, the duration of a patient's quarantine time in the hospital varies dramatically. Some patients leave the hospital after only a few days and come back daily for a check-up. Other patients need to be in the hospital for months. We'll just have to see in my case how it plays out. Dr. Lowe doesn't recommend my having the Kyphoplasty procedure so close to my stem cell transplant. Well if he doesn't recommend that I go ahead, I'll think about it, but my back hurts so much that I'm still trying to make it work.

I've been outed! My transplant doctor (Dr. Short) didn't like the fact that I was trying to get the Kyphoplasty done before the stem cell transplant, so he told the hospital where I was going to have the Kyphoplasty and they decided that it is best if I wait until after my transplant to have the procedure. There's nothing I can do about it now. Hopefully, it won't be more than four months after my transplant, because my back is really bothering me. When I do go in for my transplant, no one can stay in my room overnight while I'm quarantined. I expected that. I think it's a bigger deal for my family than me. The hospital doesn't want to take a chance with patients on that wing of the hospital catching any viruses or any other illnesses from family members.

Chapter Twenty Six

Stem Cell Transplant

January 14, 2004. Today is the day. I go through the whole nine yards for admission. The transplant unit is segregated from the rest of the hospital to ensure that patients don't develop an infection, since the immune system will be almost non-existent for a period of time. There is a special air flow system in the unit, which is supposed to filter the air more than the rest of the hospital. There is a big yellow sign on the unit door that states it must be kept closed at all times. The doctor's scheduling nurse makes it very clear to me that precautions are in force and that the staff does follow them to the letter. Masks, gowns, and gloves are required to be worn by everyone visiting so they don't transfer germs to the patients. I get the feeling that this place is going to be more rigid than the hospital across town. I'm hoping I don't have to be here very long. Who can say?

This wing of the hospital is fairly new and it has that new look. My room is a lot smaller than my rooms at the other hospital, but I get my own shower in the room, and I'll take that trade-off any day. The room has a view of the lower rooftop with those small black gravel rocks and a partial view of a college running track about a quarter of a mile away. I wonder how I will feel after the transplant and whether I will feel like looking at the outside world.

Dr. Short and the nurse practitioner come in and talk about the process. Some of my family is in the room as well. The picc line will be put in today, which is Wednesday, and then the IV of saline to hydrate me will be inserted. The chemotherapy will be given tonight. He wasn't kidding when he explained that the process was going to happen fairly quickly.

I will be getting a chemo drug called Melphalan, right before my transplant. Dr. Short described it as "wicked stuff" and said it is used in conjunction with transplant medications. It's going to kill all the cancer cells it can find and pretty much eliminate my immune system temporarily. Something that strong has to have some "wicked" side effects that I have not yet experienced.

Dr. Short indicated that I could possibly get mouth sores, lose my appetite, become agitated and nauseated, not be able to sleep, and have hot and cold flashes. He had told me about this at a prior appointment and I didn't pay that much attention then, but when it is actually time to see what happens it is more nerve racking. He had also told me that my hair would fall out, so I decided not to wait for that to happen and had the barber shave all my hair off. So I'm already at the no- hair stage with a little stubble.

The nurse, who specializes in putting in the picc line, came in once I'm settled in. The whole process takes about five minutes if everything goes well, but something isn't going right this time. The nurse can tell the line isn't going up my arm towards my neck. It doesn't feel right to her even after a couple of tries, so we go to plan B.

They took me down to radiology, where they can see how the line is going into my arm and up towards my neck on a TV monitor. The camera is right in my face. I can't even move my head while I'm lying on the table. The procedure takes about a half hour and I'm glad when it's over because my back was sore lying on that table.

They began to administer the Melphalan chemo drug on Wednesday afternoon, six hours after the IV saline was done, and it will take around three days for the side effects to kick in.
I didn't feel any different right away after they started the drug. I had taken Dexamethazone, the night before so I could get a good night's sleep before all the fun started. The "Dex" would decrease my auto-immune response.

The nurse administered Lasix in conjunction with the Melphalan to keep the kidneys moving. I took the pills a few at a time, because if I took them all at once, my stomach would get upset and I could vomit them up, defeating the purpose of taking the pills to begin with.

The nurse practitioner makes it clear that I am in charge of my case. Yeah, I think that's true. But I usually listen to people in my family when it comes to anything I need to know about when dealing with the staff. I like to think that there is less chance of something being missed with five sisters and my Mum watching out for me, God love 'em.

Dr. Short is a big Notre Dame and Chicago Bears football fan and he lets me know it. I'm wearing my Tennessee Volunteer's football t-shirt and he is kidding me about wearing it and that I should be on board with Notre Dame. The truth is I am a Notre Dame fan, but I don't tell him that. Every time he comes into my room he kids me about my shirt, but in the end I'll have the last laugh.

January 15, 2004. By Thursday, I am done with the chemo infusion, thank God. My sisters were doing their best to push the rules about not being allowed to stay overnight. The nurses said family couldn't have cots in the room, so my family figured out that the chair by the bed folds out and they would sleep there, if they could get away with it. Julie stayed until 11:30 p.m. last night.

One of the effects of the chemo is that it makes me grouchy. I didn't want to hear anyone ask me how I'm feeling today because they weren't going to like my answer. There's a lounge just down the hallway, so Sue thinks it'll do me good to go down there to sit and read and get out of my small room. She brought me today's local newspaper and the USA Today paper, like she did when I was in the hospital before. The nurses said I could take a sleeping pill tonight if I want, since I didn't sleep well last night.

January 16, 2004. This is the day me and my family have been looking forward to for a year and a half! I figure I'll take a shower this morning and maybe I'll feel better, though I doubt it. I take one anyway making sure to keep my arm elevated and not to get any water on my picc line. House- keeping comes in to change the bedding and clean up the room, so it's as clean as it can possibly be before the infusion.

The nurse in charge comes in to give me directions on the infusion. A lab person will bring in my stem cells, which have been stored and frozen since they were collected. They will either be thawed or else the doctor will thaw them in the room. The cells were washed to remove as much preservatives from them as possible. The preservatives are what cause the side effects from the infusion. A separate IV line will be put into the picc line to be used for the infusion. Dr. Short will use a huge syringe to get the cells started through the line. It will take about fifteen minutes to get all the cells into my body. I am praying that only good cells will be going back into my body and will multiply. The nurses will monitor me every five minutes initially and then every 15 minutes.

The staff reminded me about the side effects that I may experience after the infusion. My mouth and throat may develop "thrush", which is where your mouth feels like it is full of canker sores and you have a sore throat, which feels like it is burning ten times worse than the worst strep throat you have ever had. This is a result of the Melphalan, the infusion, and how all this affects my immune system. It will hurt to drink, eat, swallow and talk. They say it is supposed to last for a few days after it appears. I'll believe that when I see it. I may experience hot and cold flashes and they wanted to make sure that I would ask for extra blankets if I needed them. I knew I would get irritable and could possibly lose my temper with the staff or family, but I was the one laying in this bed, not them. I was not looking forward to not being able to get enough sleep. That just compounds all the bad side affects even more.

My family, which was out in the waiting area, said a prayer asking that the transplant be successful. I never thought it would be unsuccessful. When they brought my cells in I looked at the bag and thought there is my lifeline. The cells had already been thawed and they started the infusion. It was sort of anti-climatic when the infusion was done. I had worked very hard for a year and a half to be healthy enough to have the transplant and it was done in an hour. Now my body needs to take the good cells and MULTIPLY!

Chapter Twenty Seven

Transplant Hell

Dr. Short told me "not to push it today" because he knew what I was in store for. Within 2 hours of the infusion I became nauseated and started to vomit. The nurse practitioner came in and explained what was happening to my body. The nausea and vomiting were caused by the Melphalan, as well as a result of my cells dying. That drug IS wicked. My sister Peg knew the side effects of Melphalan and told the rest of the family what to expect, but she did not tell me. I am sure she didn't want to scare the hell out of me. The Melphalan will be flushed out of my system within 48 hours. The saline infusions will be continued to keep me hydrated and to force my kidneys to flush out any residue of the chemo.

The nurses gave me saltine crackers to help settle my stomach, but that didn't help. I even tried my good old standby oatmeal and I couldn't keep that down either. I was thirsty and drank some warm water and vomited that up as well. I was thinking that I would have to feel this lousy or worse for how many days? This sucks! What did I do to deserve this? My back pain has been manageable, but it feels worse when I'm sick like this. My body started to feel sore all over.

The family was out in the waiting area and they began to come in my room one at a time for a short visit and to let me know they were there. You don't feel so alone if you know family is right outside your door, ready to help with anything. I can't seem to fall asleep, even with the sleeping pill. It's after midnight and the hospital is normally quiet at this time, unless a nurse comes in to check on the IV's or if there are any problems. I hope I can fall asleep the next few nights or I will really be as grumpy as a bear.

January 17, 2004. I wake up at 5:15 am, 4.5 hours sleep. I hope I can get a nap today. It's my Mum's birthday, Happy Birthday Mum!

Dr. Short said the chemo effects would "hit me" on the third day and he was right. Saturday afternoon I started to feel more intense affects in a hurry. Dr. Short said this feeling would go on for the next ten days. My stomach is upset and I can't keep my food down. I try to eat any bland food I can think of that might stay down- unsalted crackers, chicken soup, popsicles, oatmeal, applesauce- but none of it is working. I still got sick on whatever I ate and I wanted to eat. My body's reaction to the transplant is turning out to be a lot worse than I'd thought it would be, and I'd thought it would be bad. I can't even keep down the fifteen pills a day that they give me. It just isn't working.

I began to experience more hot and cold flashes. I would cover up and then I would feel like my body was on fire and kick the covers off. I couldn't get comfortable and was getting grouchier. I was thirsty but was afraid to drink water or Seven Up, knowing that I would vomit it up.

Since I could not get comfortable in bed I forced myself to walk out in the hall three times a day as far as the doors to the transplant area marked: "patients do not go beyond this point". Maybe the walking would help me sleep. Like all the other patients on this wing, I was required to wear a hospital gown, gloves and a mask whenever I left my room. My immune system was very low, so it made sense to take extra precautions. I'm hooked up to the IV machine the whole time so when I leave my room I need to push it along, which isn't a big deal.

There was always one of my family members there with me. It must have driven them crazy when I would ask them to put more blankets on me and five minutes later kick them off. My body was in a tail spin and there was nothing I could do about it. My temperature would go up and down, which apparently was normal. But for me I always felt that it could be another infection like I had experienced over the last year and a half. I try to keep to my routine of walking whether or not I have an upset stomach. I need to get out of that room during the day. It makes the day go by faster. Normally I look forward to eating meals, but now, even though I still try to eat something every meal in order to keep up my caloric intake, I can't keep anything down long enough to digest. The nurse gave me some Dolasetron for the nausea but it doesn't help.

I needed to gargle with salt water solution six times a day if I didn't want the mouth sores to get worse. The salt water tastes terrible, but that's what I have to do. My brothers and sisters are doing their best to push the rules about staying overnight. They realize how important it is for me mentally to have one of them here. Going through this is very difficult. I can't imagine someone doing this by themselves.

January 18, 2004. It's my Dad's birthday. Happy birthday Dad! My Mum and Dad's birthdays are a day apart, go figure. My body is handling the treatment the best it can, but my back for some reason has been very sore since I've been in here, perhaps because of all the medications I'm taking. My Mum stops in for a short visit just as my brother Tomas leaves. My sister Mary was going to come in to sit with me, but I called and told her not to bother, because it's too cold and everything's under control.

January 19, 2004. My mouth is getting more sores, oooooh no! I need to brush all over with a toothbrush to make sure everything gets a good cleaning. Man, this smarts. I thought I was doing everything to stop this from happening, so I hope this extra cleaning prevents it from getting any worse. My blood counts are starting to drop today, and they'll go down for the next day or two, bottoming out by Wednesday and then slowly starting to come back up.

Dr. Short came in today and said I'd be staying in the hospital longer than expected. I wasn't too upset. I expected to have to stay in the hospital longer. My lungs aren't sounding the best and even if I was discharged right this minute I'd still have to come back in every day for a checkup, so what's the point. I can make it for the two long weeks I'm scheduled in the transplant wing. It has been snowing almost every day so I don't mind being here. At least I don't have to be outside shoveling.

By now I pretty much know what food my stomach can handle without getting upset. For instance, I can chew on graham crackers when I take my meds and sip on water throughout the day. Everything is going according to the plan. I don't have any side effects beyond the normal ones from the chemo and the other meds so I'm thankful for that. I noticed when I sat by the window, which is on the west side of the room, that the window and the wall below it are cold all day, so my Mum said we need to pull the shade down at the end of the day. It sounds good to me. Who am I to argue with her?

January 20, 2004. Today is my Mum and Dad's fifty third wedding anniversary. Happy Anniversary Mum and Dad!

The doctor came in today and explained the timeline for the coming days. My red blood cells counts will be at their lowest levels in the next couple of days and then slowly start to climb. He also says that the face masks don't really work for people coming in the room and visiting. The masks get wet from the person's saliva. He advised that if someone feels sick, they should stay away altogether for now. My lungs are crackling when he listens to them, so he wants me to sit in the chair and not on my bed. I've also been ordered by my sisters to blow in the spirometer regularly. So, when I'm not rinsing out my mouth throughout the day or blowing in the tube, I'm walking out in the hall. I try to eat but I don't have much of an appetite. I drink as much water as I can, but with the saline I'm not that thirsty.

January 22, 2004. By day seven the doctor gives me an option. I can check out right now and come back every day for a check-up or stay in the hospital for another week. On the one hand, I'd be out of the hospital and away from the routine. On the other hand, we'd have to travel 45 minutes to get here every day for a check-up. I don't want to have to travel or have my parents drive all the way here, not knowing what the weather would be like, when I could just stay here for precaution's sake for another week. Another option I had was to rent a hotel room just down the block and come back every day, as some patients do. But I'll be less likely to have complications if I was already in here or if I did develop a problem, I'd be right here already. So, I decided to stay in the hospital for another week. It'll go by fast, the worst was almost over.

My brother Tomas and my sister Trish would always be messing with the nursing staff as their idea of a joke. When someone would come in to get some blood samples, they would tell that person that someone had already been in and taken blood just an hour ago, which wasn't true. The nurse would go check the chart and see that it was more like four hours ago. Finally, one of the more experienced nurses' caught on to the two of them and said she knows they were messing with her and the other nurses, so they were found out. A little humor everyday helps!

It feels like I've been here two weeks instead of only seven days. My white blood cell count and platelets and other numbers are all dropping. I'm nauseous today, as usual, and I'm doing my same routine. My mouth is okay, but I don't have much of an appetite. Tomorrow I'll be getting a platelet transfusion. I'm not having a reaction to any medications, so I expect to handle the transfusion ok. I've had three doctors check in on me, and one of them tells me that the nausea and other symptoms are normal, because my GI tract is affected by the chemo, and my immune system (white blood cell count) is low, which doesn't help in the recovery process. I'm getting to sleep late at night even with a sleeping pill and I'm waking up early. I've got too much energy, even with being sick. Yeah, this is why people don't like hospitals, no sleep.

January 23, 2004. It's Friday and my sister Sue stops by. She brought me two newspapers. I was checking out all the stories written about the Super Bowl. It helps to pass the time. My body felt colder than normal because my blood level was low, so we turned up the thermostat. A male nurse came in to give me a neupogen shot, which stimulates the body to create more white blood cells. I've had this shot the last four days. I ordered oatmeal today, hoping I could keep it down, but no such luck. Oh well, we can cross oatmeal off the list.

I developed a temperature late last night of 101, which is to be expected, and I feel terrible. They must have wanted to make sure that I wasn't getting pneumonia because the nurses took a chest x-ray last night at 1:30 am. I did sleep pretty well for the first time in several days. I'm taking Tylenol for the pain in my back and for the fever. My mouth sores are not any worse, and my lungs sound good. I'm still using the spirometer. How could I not with five sisters, a Mum and Dad, and two brothers giving it to me all the time? I hate that device and I hate the person who invented it.

January 24, 2004. I'm fatigued from not eating and not sleeping consistently. I can't wait to get out of here! One of the doctors' stops in and tells me I should start to feel better in a couple of days. Oh really? We'll see about that, doctor. The doctor is going to prescribe Vancomycin for the elevated temperature and hopefully it'll do the trick.

I've lost some weight since I've been in here, which is understandable. The picc line is likely to come out soon as bacteria appears to have colonized somewhere on the line. Both of the blood cultures came back positive yesterday for bacterial infection. One blood culture tests the picc line and the other tests the peripheral blood. The nurses will take another blood culture today. I'm still taking Tylenol for the fever and headaches, and it helps a little bit. The nurses put lorazapam in my picc line for the nausea. Fifteen minutes later they took out the line.

January 26, 2004. The precautions have been removed. No more gloves or gowns needed to be worn by visitors. My white blood cell count is rising, which means the stem cells are working. The more my white blood cell count rises, the better I'll feel, and the vomiting and the nausea will improve.

Chapter Twenty Eight

Breaking Out

January 30, 2004. The blood draw is an every morning occurrence. It's annoying but what are you going to do? Just get it over with and move on. The pain in my back today is between two and three. My numbers continue to slowly rise. I've been in here for two weeks and today my prayers are answered. The nurse just came in and informed me that I'll be released from the hospital today. I'm breaking out of this joint! My numbers are obviously good enough and my white blood cells are coming up to the point where I can recover at home. As usual with discharges, they give me general rules to follow when I'm at home, so my recovery will continue. Yeah, that's what I have five sisters for. They, along with my Mum, remind me of those rules. A nurse tells me my next checkup was in a week, and then we signed the papers and I was wheeled down to the exit and got into the van. The biting winter wind of the Midwest never felt so good. I love it! Call me crazy, but just for one day.

The best thing about getting out of the hospital is you don't have to follow the hospital's daily schedule. I get to sleep in my own bed and eat my Mum's cooking. I needed to get some home cooking since I wasn't eating in the hospital and lost at least 12 pounds. I just had to watch what I eat because my stomach was so messed up from all the vomiting. Mum's spaghetti is going to have to wait a few weeks until my stomach could handle it.

The standard timeframe they gave for transplant recovery was it could take up to a year for this kind of transplant, but that's playing it safe. I'm not going to walk on the treadmill for the first week, but after that I'll be back on it for sure. I needed to eat six times a day if I wanted to gain my weight back, and I think I could handle my Mum's food that many times a day; you don't even have to force me.

Recovering from a stem cell transplant is about a routine. I needed to go in for a checkup every two weeks to do labs, have a chest x-ray, and ask/answer any questions. This first week back home I stayed true to my word. I just walked around the house and stayed inside to be cautious. My appetite started to come back, I was feeling stronger and my mood was better, which my family was happy about. My latest labs showed my red blood cell count is back to normal at 4.4 (normal 4.4-5.8), white blood cell count is 3.7 (normal 3.8-10.5), and platelets are 148 (normal 160-370). I feel good and everything is going according to schedule. The one thing I realized with all my medical issues is if you're not moving forward then you're going backwards and I was hoping to avoid that.

I'm anxious to move ahead and deal with my back issues. I knew going in that the transplant wasn't going to be the biggest medical decision I'd have to make. The transplant turned out to be more difficult to get through than I thought it would be, but nonetheless I am looking ahead after getting out of the hospital.

Dr. Short is responsible for my case for one hundred days following the transplant date discharge, a 100 day post transplant contract. But I wanted to push the envelope to see if I can get in to have the Kyphoplasty procedure which is minor surgery, just under 100 days from the day of discharge. It would be the first week of April if I can get the doctor to approve and sign off on it. At first he says it's alright so I naturally go ahead and get it set up with the hospital that will be doing the Kyphoplasty procedure. But when the hospital contacts Dr. Short to let him know what is going to take place and when, he said no to that timeline. Boy was I upset. I knew he must have forgotten what the timeline was but I was still upset in getting my hopes up and then saying no.

I can understand where he was coming from. He was responsible for my case for this time frame and if something were to happen, he'd be liable; so I had to go along with his decision. I guess my Mum summed it up best. I was tired of wearing the back brace and I didn't want to have to wear it for the rest of my life.

Days drifted into weeks and then months. I needed to be a little patient, and it'll be here before I know it. My post transplant recovery was going off without a hitch, no infections or colds. But I couldn't help thinking that something had to go wrong. This was going too well. Exercising, eating right, and becoming stronger and healthier were my goals.

Dr. Short made the point that the coagulant aspect had to be leveled whenever invasive incisions are involved. My present INR was elevated as well, which means my blood was not at the right level and I could have a blood clot during surgery, if the level wasn't at the right stage. So he worked with me in getting my blood levels where they needed to be before the surgery.

Once he gave me the go ahead to schedule the Kyphoplasty I didn't waste any time contacting the hospital that would do the procedure. My insurance company wasn't going to pay for the procedure. It was out of my insurance network, and no doctors in the area did this procedure. So I was going to have to foot the bill if I wanted the procedure. If that's what I had to do then I had to do it. I don't care how much it costs. I'd find a way to pay for it. I can't put a price tag on the pain in my back, and I don't want to be bent over for the rest of my life.

Chapter Twenty Nine

Kyphoplasty

In order to make an initial appointment with the spinal surgeon I had to pay for the entire procedure up front. The price of the procedure would cost around $5,000 and I decided to put it on my credit card. The hospital would end up charging my insurance 4 times that if the procedure were finally approved.

I was lucky enough to get an appointment with a spinal surgeon who was trained by the doctor I had seen last year out of state. I'm thinking if he was trained by that surgeon, then he probably worked on cases similar to mine and was taught by the best. He had a long last name that I could not pronounce so I just called him Dr. K.

My pre-op appointment was to meet Dr. K., go over my history and labs, and have some skeletal x-rays taken. Some of my family came to the appointment and was able to ask their questions. I had been through so many things the last couple of years, I felt it was important for the family to understand the procedure and feel more in the know ahead of time. After reviewing my x-rays he said he felt this procedure could provide me some relief and he was willing to perform the surgery. He gave me information to read and we scheduled it for June. I finally felt that we were moving forward now.

June 2004. The Kyphoplasty surgery day is here. I'm more excited than nervous. The procedure would be on an out-patient basis. If I needed to stay overnight in the hospital I would, but otherwise I could go home. Would I be able to walk out of the hospital after the procedure and not need to wear the brace? That was the big question for me.

The Kyphoplasty procedure would begin with Dr. K. injecting a balloon into the vertebrae area. Then he would inflate the balloon and inject "cement like substance" into the areas of the vertebrae that had worn down and was pinching the spinal nerves, thereby causing pain. The procedure attempts to restore the spine to its original shape as best it could. This is all accomplished with the aid of a camera that is attached at the end of the device used for the procedure. In my case, Dr. K. would be assisted by a technical rep from the company that provides the "cement like substance" for the procedure. His role was to provide guidance for the surgeon if he had any questions about the device or the substance used while the procedure was being done. The procedure could take anywhere from an hour to several hours, depending on the number and severity of vertebrae that needed to be fixed.

The day of the procedure we got to the hospital early and were directed to the day surgery unit. I was taken to a prep room and my family was directed to a specific waiting area, since there were so many of them. After getting into the hospital gown, a nurse took me to a small room and inserted an IV for saline and some medication that would put me to sleep during the operation. When I got on the surgery table they wanted me to lie on my stomach the whole time. I don't know how this was going to work. I don't normally lie on my stomach at all. So I just relaxed and hoped the "knockout gas" would do the trick. One problem with my lying on my stomach was that I couldn't extend my right arm over my head and place it on the table, due to a previous shoulder injury. The nurse seemed unhappy when I told her this but that was tough. They would just have to make it work by partially extending my right arm. It was uncomfortable, but I figure I could deal with it for the procedure. The areas of my back that the doctor would be working on were the thoracic (middle) and the lumbar (lower).

It didn't take long for me to fall asleep. I was asleep for about forty-five minutes and then three quarters of the way through the procedure I started to wake up. I could hear Dr. K. asking the tech support person about the area he was currently working on. The doctor was looking through a screen that showed where he was in my spine with the wand that injects the solution into the vertebrae. As I woke up and became semi-conscious, I could feel the doctor working on my spine, and it hurt like hell. He could see that I'm awake but I don't tell him how much I was hurting because I didn't want him to stop until he had done as much as he could. So when he asked how I was doing, I said I was fine, and he kept working. The last forty-five minutes went really slow. I told myself to relax and it would be over shortly. I was so glad when he finally finished.

Ironically, the tech rep who was advising Dr. K. was a guy I knew from college. I don't remember his name, but he looked familiar. It was a small college, and I knew I had played pickup basketball with him once in a while.

Once the procedure was finished, the nurses carefully turned me over, and it felt so good to be lying on my back. The nurses carefully wheeled me out and into a recovery room. The main nurse wanted me to sit up in bed at a certain angle, so the substance wouldn't develop any complications. Already, I felt as if some of the discomfort had left my body. I noticed that I was sitting up straighter, and my family noticed too when they came into the room. I was hoping to go home later today if my recovery went well. After three hours the nurse in charge of my care said they were going to release me soon. SWEET! I could feel the improvement in my spine already. My sternum felt like it was no longer resting near my lungs when I took a deep breath now. I didn't have as much pain.

Nonetheless, checking out of the hospital was an effort in patience since the nurse was nowhere to be found. All I could do was wait. My Dad drove us cautiously and carefully home with pillows around my back, because my family was concerned that my back was still unstable so soon after the procedure. But I feel fine. I feel a lot better after the procedure, so yeah, it was a success!

Things were moving in the right direction regarding my health. First the stem cell transplant went well and now the Kyphoplasty procedure had gone well. So I'm celebrating the success but tempering my enthusiasm because this isn't a sprint it's an ultra marathon, and I know it needs to continue. The next day you move on to what's next. As my brother-in-law Andy says "I have been compartmentalizing each phase of my marathon."

Dr. K. told me that it would take more than one Kyphoplasty procedure to get the best possible results in my case. He said he wanted to see how the spine adjusts to the first procedure, but that the second procedure wouldn't be nearly as long or as detailed. Based on how the first one went, I decided to go back for a second procedure. I knew I would be a lot more prepared, having gone through it once and knowing now what to expect. Dr. K. was only going to work on three vertebrae at a time, so he still had three left to do. He decided that the three in the cervical area of my neck were too risky to attempt.

The second procedure couldn't be done for three months, so in the meantime, I continued to see Dr. Lowe for my scheduled appointments, taking my medication, exercising, and trying to stay healthy. I knew the Kyphoplasty procedure was a short-term solution for my back and sternum issues, but it felt good to get some positive results. It lifted my spirits, and I think it lifted my families as well, especially my Mum and Dad.

Chapter Thirty

Round Two

Trying to get in to see a spinal surgeon isn't an easy appointment to make. They're usually backed up for two to three months and I have to stand in line and take a number. The problem isn't getting approval for an appointment by my insurance. It was getting an appointment with the surgeon. I was able to schedule my second procedure for the end of August. Now I needed to stay healthy and be patient.

August 28, 2004. It had been three months since my first Kyphoplasty procedure, and I'm ready for the second one. I know what to expect so I'm not as nervous this time. The area of my spine Dr. K. is going to operate on is the lower (lumbar) part of my back. I guess we will see how much it helps. With the first procedure I had immediate results in alleviating some pain and I am hopeful that will be the case with the second. They must have adjusted the amount of anesthesia they used this time, because I was unconscious the whole time. The results from the second procedure weren't quite as noticeable as the first. Dr. K. had done about as much as he was willing to do. The results were what I expected, a success, but it was a short-term solution for a bigger problem with my sternum and the area of my cervical spine that was painful.

Outcomes during doctor appointments can change in a hurry for the worse. I've experienced it firsthand. I was out in the reception area waiting to see the doctor for my three month check up. A patient, who was sitting right next to me, had received bad news after her blood tests were reviewed. The nurse came out to clarify some things for her and explained what her next steps would be. The patient was obviously in shock.

As I was walking in for my appointment another oncology doctor was already sitting with her to check on her and provide some comfort. During my appointment I couldn't help but think of what that woman must have been thinking of at that moment. You think everything is going okay one minute and then lightning strikes. A person can only imagine how a diagnosis like this changes your life until it happens to you. Your life priorities change to your health and survival.

I've heard so many different conversations from patients out in the waiting area. It sounds like a therapy session. One day as I was in for a checkup, this person was talking about her breast cancer experience. The person across the way talked about losing her eyebrows during her chemotherapy treatment. Another patient talked about having the cancer come back for the second time. Waiting for another appointment, a lady sitting across from me was just diagnosed and going to see her doctor for the first time. The other patients in the waiting area reassured her that the doctor she is seeing is very good. Her doctor is the same doctor as I have, Dr. Lowe.

Everybody in the waiting area that I have ever seen and listened to seems to be at ease around other patients who they can relate to. I'm numb to all the stories now. I think I'm just a lot more tolerant of reacting to someone else's medical problems.

I just had a friend, who went up to the Mayo clinic in Minnesota for an all important check-up. This was a big deal because it would tell her how her body was doing as a result of the medications she was taking. They went to the Mayo clinic because that was the only hospital that had a clinical trial for this patient's disease. You have to go where you can find the best chance for positive results for your survival and my friend's best chance for success was participating in this clinical trial.

It was a long trip from where my friend was traveling to the clinic, but you can bet she and her family was thinking about all the possible outcomes from the tests. I know because I've been down that road many times. You can't make a big deal about it but it is the biggest test you'll ever take in your life and the results could change your life drastically. You do all you can to keep your mind busy and off the upcoming appointment, but the closer you come to the time the more anxious and nervous you become. Thinking about it doesn't help; it only makes the appointment seem worse than it already is. If you do all you can for your health and you follow your treatment course there's nothing more that you can do. The hundreds of appointments you'll have in your lifetime will become less nerve racking. Trust me, the anxiety and nervousness will wear off, at least it has for me.

I heard from my friend on the way back from her appointment that the news was good. The lab tests showed that the disease was in remission and the treatment was moving along as well as could be expected. Good news is always a reason to celebrate the moment, so they went out and celebrated.

I'd be lying if I said all my appointments went well. You have to try and be on an even keel when you go in because you could get bad news and then you have to deal with it, make some quick decisions and move on. I think about my disease almost every day, but I don't worry about it. My worrying is not going to make it any better for myself. My family and friends are not going to be any better off either if I lay all my concerns on their doorstep. I don't see any benefit in talking about my concerns with them anyway. They have their own personal issues to deal with on a daily basis.

I read a quote by Bobby Bowden, the former head football coach at Florida State University, which has always stuck with me. He said "Ninety-eight percent of the public don't want to hear about your problems, and the other two percent are glad you have them and they don't." I thought it was a funny quote, but the more I thought about it the more I think it's true. Everyone has problems big and small and to each person theirs are most important.

I don't believe people want to hear details of anyone else's medical issues, let alone mine. The only time my health comes up in conversation is in small talk when people ask "how I'm feeling today." If others don't bring it up, I don't bring it up. It's just easier for everybody. They don't feel uncomfortable and I don't feel uncomfortable having to explain, enough said.

A friend introduced me to a woman, who had just successfully completed a kidney transplant, and my friend filled her in on my medical history. I don't like to get into a conversation about my medical background with a stranger, but I tried to make the best of it. They were asking about my medications - how many pills I was taking - and I knew where this was going. The woman was comparing her medical situation to mine. She said she couldn't believe I was taking fewer medications for my cancer than she was following a kidney transplant. By her tone of voice she didn't believe that was right. I knew what she was getting at by remarks like that, which is the reason I don't get into medical conversations with anybody. When people want to talk about their medical situation, I don't have a problem with listening and empathizing with them. Often they just want to talk to someone, just to get it off their chest. But no two medical histories are exactly alike, so I don't look for any similarities between other peoples' stories and mine.

I never wanted to take the chance of worsening my condition by not taking my medications regularly. I've spent a lot of money on medications and I'm thankful that they're doing the job. I just bite the bullet and tell myself that my health is worth it. The pharmacy techs at the drugstore act surprised when they have to tell me how much my medications are going to cost, and I tell them I already know. My Thalidomide is expensive even with insurance here in the United States. What? Should I stop taking it because of the price, even though it works? Nothing doing. I worked too hard to get where I am now to take the chance. The consequences could be terrible in the long run. I do what I have to do to survive, plain and simple.

I started taking Thalidomide when I was first diagnosed and, at the time, I didn't know that my insurance didn't cover it. It cost $ 2000 a month. Sue, who is my financial power of attorney, was smart not to tell me back then that I was paying for it out of my own pocket. I probably would have freaked out, and I didn't need that stress about money. Because really, what did money matter? I needed the medication, period. I later found out that Sue had contacted the drug company and found out they had a program that assisted people in paying lower amounts for their drug. Persistence pays off.

Chapter Thirty One

Jumping Through Hoops

September 20, 2004. I was finally able to get in and see one of the top spinal surgeons in our area. Most of my sisters and both of my parents were squeezed into the exam room for this appointment. When the doctor and his associate open the door, I can see they are surprised that it's standing room only in here. But the doctor doesn't have a problem with it, and I don't either, so let's get on with the appointment. First, he looked at my most recent x-rays and then discussed the options with his colleague. I am not having a good feeling about their conversation.

He had me stand, examined my back, and asked several questions about my illness and the medications I am taking. The bottom line is that he will not attempt the type of surgery I need. He feels the risks are too great. The biggest concern, he told us, is that the surgery would be so close to my spinal cord and that the possible damage, in a worse - case scenario, could leave me paralyzed. He asks if I take pain medication and I say "Only when I need to, not that often." Like he thinks I should get used to taking pain medication for the rest of my life. He isn't going to attempt the procedure, so he's giving me his opinion on an alternative. No thanks. I feel especially bad about my family having to sit in on this consult and hear him say no to any surgery options. The truth is I didn't want him to do it anyway. I just needed him to say he refuses so I can go on to the next doctor in the area and have him deny me, and then be denied by the next doctor, etc.

My insurance isn't going to cover any surgery out of my insurance network unless I see everybody in the area who is qualified and get a no answer. I'm going to have to jump through all the hoops to get where I want to go, and I am willing to do it.

I've already decided that I want and need Dr. Man, the surgeon Julie and I went to see in Cleveland, to do the surgery. No spinal surgeon in my network has any experience with my type of case. I know this and my family knows this. Now, walking out of this meeting with the top spinal surgeon in the area, at least we've heard his opinion and asked questions about his concerns. I am disappointed, yes, but I'm not discouraged. I'm not giving up. The surgeon I just saw was trained by Dr. Man, the surgeon I wanted all along. So this is a start, getting a first letter denying the surgery. It has to do with my insurance, so this is what I have to do. There are three hospitals in my area and all the spinal surgeons that could possibly do my surgery were at the same hospital. So I would be getting the same response from all the surgeons.

October 18, 2004. I've been assigned a case manager from the insurance company, and this person informs my sister Sue, through a series of e-mails, the name of the doctor who assesses my case for the insurance company. I guess you can say he's an advisor for the insurance company and makes recommendations based on his consults with doctors about particular surgeries and other procedures patients want to have.

My first bill from the hospital where I had the Kyphoplasty procedure done comes to Sue, who is my financial power of attorney. My insurance denies coverage of the bill, which amounts to just under $20,000.00. The doctor from the insurance company had consulted with the top spinal surgeon in my insurance network in the area.

Since my spinal condition has changed, the case manager now recognizes Kyphoplasty as a covered procedure if done within their network. But what if no one in the area is qualified and I'm not satisfied with their ability to perform the procedure?

Am I then bound to have a doctor I don't have confidence in to do the procedure just because he/she is covered by my insurance to do it? How can I be assured that they'll do the best job possible on my spine? Well I can't.

I called the local spine surgeon's office to schedule an appointment to discuss the pain in my back, which is getting worse. The scheduling person is abrupt on the phone, telling me that everyone who calls the office complains of pain and that the soonest that they can get me in for an appointment is the end of the month. The scheduling receptionist also indicates that they would not be giving me a referral to have a procedure done at the out of network hospital. It is none of her business how and where my medical treatment is done. Clearly, I'm going to have to jump through hoops to get the insurance company to decide that this procedure is possible and warranted. But you know what? I don't care, I'll wear them down. The insurance company and their doctors are going to give up on my case long before I do, I assure you. They don't know yet who they're dealing with. They haven't seen the smoke coming out of my sister's ears. I had no idea until recently that e-mails had been sent to my sisters regarding the process of my insurance claims and the denials. I am concerned about my back, period, and I'd deal with any and everything that went along with it if I had too.

In their denial, the insurance company claims that my requests were received too late, even though pre-authorizations were requested by me many weeks prior to the actual appointments. But that's from their point of view. The bottom line is their possible solution is not the best possible solution for my spine. If I don't take the appointment with the local surgeon, is the insurance company going to say they offered me a solution and they have the leverage to deny me coverage? Who is the unbiased doctor within the insurance network to say what the best possible solution is for me, ignoring the financial aspects?

Mary and Sue are both dealing extensively with the case manager. Mary has on-going conversations with the case manager regarding this entire process, and Sue most often deals with billing issues. It makes it easier for all of us when the insurance company and the case manager deal with only one or two people and then the information is shared with the rest of the family.

The insurance company sent us a copy of the hospital billing charges for the second Kyphoplasty procedure: $2,100.00. Consult from last November: $294.00. X-rays: $2500.00. In the end, I may have to pay for the surgery out of my pocket. Am I willing to accept the risk of a somewhat less experienced but highly skilled surgeon within my insurance network to do my surgeries? Ah, no! The consult with a patient shows he has a personal investment in the outcome of the surgery. I'd try to get the doctor's insight into my case. I want all the doctors I talk with at these consults to open up to what is their thinking and how he would answer these questions.

Even though I knew he'd almost certainly turn me down, I make an appointment with the second most qualified surgeon in the area. I send in my x-rays and wait three months to see him. I don't want to see him; I just need him to deny me and give me a letter for the insurance company.

A few days before the appointment I got a letter from this surgeon saying that he reviewed my x-rays and records and won't attempt the procedure. Great! That saved me and my family the drive to the appointment. I'm disappointed for about as long as it takes to read the letter, and then turn my attention toward getting back in touch with the spinal surgeon I want to do the procedure.

I'm trying to stay positive, upbeat, and motivated during this time. It would be easy to get down after one or two doctors said no, but I have hope on my side. I don't know what it is, but I knew something good was going to happen. I don't know when, but it's going to happen. I'm exercising, eating right and being cautious with my health. Something's going to work out.

Chapter Thirty Two

There is Hope

January 14, 2005. I received a phone call on Tuesday from the Cleveland Clinic for an appointment the following Monday. It is one and a half hours to fly there and I want to fly this time. I don't want to wait any longer. I need to hear what this doctor has to say. So we go ahead and schedule the appointment on short notice. One of my many problems with going out of state to a health clinic on short notice is getting approval from the insurance company for the appointment and necessary tests. I don't have much confidence that the insurance company will approve me but the insurance company's liaison in charge of my case says she'll get an answer by Friday if we send all the paperwork to her ASAP. So we fax everything immediately. To my great surprise, they approved the appointment! I couldn't believe it but I wasn't going to argue with them. I would've gone whether they approved me or not, but this way they're saving me about a thousand dollars out of pocket.

We're flying this time, even though it's hard to find deals on airline tickets on short notice. Julie will come with me. I'd be willing to go alone, but my parents don't want that, so that's that. We'll fly out Sunday afternoon, stay overnight, go to the appointment Monday morning, and fly back Monday afternoon if all goes well. Already I'm nervous thinking about what could go wrong. What if he looks at my case and decides against it? That would be devastating to me right now. I know I'm putting all my eggs in one basket with this guy, which you shouldn't do, but he's my best shot – maybe my only shot.

January 19, 2005. We arrive at our hotel early Sunday evening, and already I'm feeling more nervous than I ever felt before. I know I'm not going to sleep much because I don't have the foam cover that I put on the bed to make it softer for my back. I don't get to bed until late and I don't sleep much. The nervous anticipation is still with me in the early morning. I'm breathing so shallow I feel short of breath all the time. I'll be better once I see the surgeon.

Everyone at our hotel is going to the clinic, and we grab one of the shuttle buses that stop by every fifteen minutes. At the building where my appointment will be we take the elevator to the fourth floor and come around the corner to the waiting area, where despite the early hour, I see close to forty people sitting in chairs. This is the biggest waiting area I've ever seen. Four receptionists are handling patients' charts and taking medical information from patients. We check in and take a seat and after a half hour of waiting they call my name. A nurse takes us down a long hallway around a corner to a waiting room. She says the doctor will be in to see you shortly, which they always say, even when they're running late. The exam room is tiny - half the size of a dorm room so they can fit lots of rooms onto this floor. I mean how big of a room do you need anyway?

Finally, after all this time and effort, I'm going to get to meet with the surgeon I want to see and get his thoughts on my case. My insurance company has already disapproved my getting all the tests I needed done here so we'd had to get the other tests done back home. The sticking point was the three dimensional x-rays that the clinic requested. I just hope the x-rays were done up to their specifications. I don't need any more delays if we can help it. Dr. Man's scheduling assistant comes in first and introduces herself. Her name is Mary Jane and she explains that she handles his scheduling of tests and makes sure all necessary tests are done before surgery. She also says she answers any and all questions families have and keeps them up to date during a surgical procedure.

Meanwhile, there are three doctors just outside the door looking over my x-rays and discussing my case. We walk past them and take a right into the exam room. I finally hear the doctors conversing outside about my case, looking at the x-rays. I know you shouldn't eavesdrop on other people's conversations but I'm trying to pick out what they were saying.

After what seems like a long time, Dr. Man comes in and introduces himself and we greet one another with handshakes and sit down to discuss my case. Dr. Man is average height, trim build and has a firm hand shake. He has a no- nonsense, let's get to the problem, personality. He definitely has an air of confidence about him as he enters the room.

He says he has heard a lot about my case and was hoping he could help me. That's all I needed to hear. The tests we had done previously for my bones and spine looked good. My bone density test shows my bones overall are strong enough for a procedure or procedures to happen. As Dr. Man talks I'm listening and concentrating but not looking him in the eye. I guess it was pretty apparent. Julie certainly noticed and brought it up after our meeting. The truth is once he said he could help me that was all I remember hearing. After about a fifteen minute discussion, we decided together where we would go from here and what I would have to do in order to go ahead with this procedure. I'll need to pass another pulmonary function test. That should be okay. I passed one previously before my stem cell transplant, so I should be able to pass one again, unless I have a setback with a lung infection.

After Dr. Man and Mary Jane left the room, Julie points out that I wasn't looking at the doctor at all while he talked to me. I agreed but I told her I heard what he said. She thinks I was disrespectful to Dr. Man and should apologize. I didn't think it was a big deal but I told her she was right.

I asked Julie to let the doctor know I wanted to see him for a moment when he got a chance. When he came back in I explained about not looking him in the eyes, and as I'm apologizing I suddenly get all choked up. I don't even know why, and I composed myself quickly. But Dr. Man didn't seem surprised. He said that patients with cancer have a lot to deal with and he understood. We shook hands and moved on.

As Julie and I were riding to the airport, I felt hopeful again. Naturally Julie needed to share the news with the family. I suppose if we didn't call them right away they would assume the appointment didn't go well, so why keep them in the dark. As I settled into the plane I'm relieved to finally have some good news for a change.

January 21, 2005. I just needed to keep doing what I am doing. I exercise daily, try to sleep regularly, eat a balanced diet, and stay away from enclosed spaces filled with people, where I'm more likely to catch a virus. That would stop my having any surgery at all. I also made an appointment for a bone density test to confirm that my bones were strong enough. A bone density tests consists of a needle being inserted either in a rib in my back or in my hip area. It's a pretty painful procedure but thank god it only takes a few seconds to complete. I've had it done before so I know what to expect. The first time I had the test I asked my brother Steve to give me his hand so I could squeeze it for the few seconds of intense pain when they inserted the needle. This time it's a lot easier since I know what the pain will be like and how long it will last.

I need my insurance company to approve the costs of the upcoming surgeries. I've been to every spine specialist in the area that the insurance company referred me to, and they all agreed that the surgery is too dangerous to attempt, which is just what I wanted to hear. I mean, would you want a surgeon to perform a risky procedure and not be a hundred percent positive about his abilities? I don't think anybody would want a surgeon who felt that way. Me, I know who and what I want and now I have to convince the insurance company to cover the cost. That will take time and patience, both of which I have.

I need to show the insurance company all the evidence we obtained from the doctors and hope they'll see it from our angle. Dr. Man has experience with patients who have spine problems along with myeloma. He's one of the inventors of the Kyphoplasty procedure and knows it better than anyone else. I couldn't ask for a better doctor in my case. Still I'm not holding my breath that the insurance company will approve of these out-of-network procedures. I've heard many stories of insurance companies turning people down in similar situations.

Unfortunately, it's impossible for me not to worry about it all the time. The worst part of my whole situation is this uncertainty, the constant suspense of waiting to hear what the insurance company will decide about my life. All I can do is try to stay positive and keep myself as healthy as I possibly can. The truth is I know what I want, and even if the insurance company won't approve it, I'm having the procedure. We'll figure out how to pay for it when the time comes. But I'm hoping it doesn't come to that.

Dr. Lowe scheduled the pulmonary function test to happen soon. It takes all day to get all the x-rays that Dr. Man has requested. For one set of x-rays, I had to lie on my stomach. I ground my teeth the whole time waiting for it to be done. The frustration in getting my surgery approved was stressing out my sisters, Mary in particular. One day Mary was at work in her company's boardroom and on the phone with Dr. Lowe when all her frustration spilled over and she started yelling into the phone " Why can't we get a piece of paper saying a doctor locally has referred Tim to this other out-of-state surgeon"? Evidently something clicked with Dr. Lowe. Perhaps he realized we were not going to give up, or maybe simply seeing that no one else was going to do anything, and he was going to be the one to step out on a limb with us. In any case, he said "I'll do it, I'll write the referral." And just like that we moved on. Mary was relentless!

My lungs weren't completely healed from the MRSA (methicillin-resistant staphylococcus), double pneumonia, lung infection, and bronchitis. The lungs could take up to a year to recover from the pneumonia, but I knew my lungs were in better shape than they were before Dr. Lowe scheduled the tests. I didn't do very well. Walking around a hallway at a fast pace was one test, and my lungs didn't sound very good when the nurse listened with a stethoscope. The second test was the pulmonary function test which was blowing into a tube. You take a deep breath in and blow out all the air you can through the tube, for as long as you can. You do this about a half dozen times, while the machine records your levels. I thought I was doing alright but the machine showed otherwise. As a result of the test, Dr. Lowe decided I needed to go back on oxygen, because my lungs would not be able to improve on their own. What a bummer. When I walked on the treadmill I liked to crank the incline to the highest level, so oxygen would really help.

Dr. Lowe suggested we switch to liquid oxygen, because it's easier to handle and the smaller fanny pack is more user-friendly than the big metal oxygen tanks.

All the requested x-rays had been completed, and I was exercising as much as I could, walking on the steep inclined treadmill daily in order to get my heart working. I'm pretty tired when I got done but I felt better.

On the day of the pulmonary test, I felt ready, but nervous and uncertain. Physically, I didn't feel any different than I did when I took the test before, and I didn't know if that was a good sign, but I did my best. Then there was the waiting, waiting and more waiting. The hospital didn't contact me directly with the results. Instead they contacted the Cleveland Clinic and the clinic called to schedule my pre-op for surgery. I guess that meant I passed the pulmonary function test. I definitely felt more nervous now knowing I'm having surgery.

Six weeks from today I was on the schedule for my first surgery. All the effort of dealing with the doctors, battling the insurance company, and struggling to get my body in shape for the surgery was going to pay off.

I never specifically asked Dr. Lowe for his approval of the surgery. He is an oncology doctor and a very good one, but this was about my spine. If he had any concerns about me having the surgery, he should have brought them up long ago. But I think he knew how determined I was and that he couldn't have changed my mind anyway. Nonetheless, he's my primary doctor and technically he could have stopped the surgery if he felt it was too dangerous. But he never did.

Meanwhile, my follow-up appointment with Dr. Man was almost upon us. I don't know where the time went, but I'm glad it was gone. We didn't plan on driving the 11 hours again and booked our flights.

Julie, Mary and my Mum flew down with me, bringing along the recent x-rays the clinic requested. We arrived the Sunday afternoon before my appointment and stayed at the hotel on the clinic campus again. Since we'd been there before we knew what to do, what bus to get on, where to get off, etc. Once again I was nervous on the morning of the appointment. In the exam room Dr. Man came in and introduced himself to my sisters, Mum, and sat down to discuss my case.

He got right down to business, saying yes he could do the surgery. He said he normally did this type of surgery on children with severe spinal abnormalities. He made it very clear that this procedure could paralyze me. He explains that I will require several procedures over three months time until he is satisfied with the outcome. He speaks very generally about the procedure, telling us that he won't know precisely what needs to be done until he gets into my body.

I don't know who was happier, me or my family, but we were all eager to hear more details from him. At this point I didn't care what I would have to go through to get this surgery started. I needed to ask him one important question. How many cases like mine had he done? He said he had done 13 procedures similar to mine, and that one patient died during surgery, an older person with more serious lung problems than mine. I didn't need to know any more about that particular case. As sad as it was to hear, this man's health wasn't going to affect my decision. Of course I understood that Dr. Man wanted to prepare me for the worst- case scenario, and he made it perfectly clear that there were risks involved, and that I could also be confined to a wheelchair for the rest of my life if something went wrong.

I asked him to repeat how many of these procedures he'd done. He repeated "I've done thirteen procedures" and then he picked up on my meaning- that thirteen was not a lucky number- so for the record he has performed either twelve or fourteen procedures. He laughed along with everyone else in the room. He wanted me to go home and think about what he had said and get back in touch with him to give him my answer about moving forward.

Walking out of there I was pretty damned happy. The appointment had gone as well as I could have hoped for, and by the time we arrived back at the hotel I'd already made my decision to go ahead with the surgeries. I asked Julie to call the doctor's office to speak to Dr. Man. He was doing rounds, so we'd call when we got back home.

Since we left the appointment pretty early we were ahead of schedule. We called the airline and learned that they had room for us on the next flight leaving in 25 minutes. It takes 20 minutes to get to the airport from the hospital, and it was raining, so I was thinking that there was no way we could make it in time. The hotel called us a cab, which showed up right away, and we all jumped into the cab.

The car is one of those older police cars with a spotlight mounted on the driver-side door and the back-end suspension raised up. I still didn't think we had a chance in hell to make that flight. When we told the driver we were in a hurry, he started driving like he was on the Sprint Cup circuit, cutting in and out of traffic in the rain. He drove right up on people's bumpers the whole way, and I was sitting in the middle of the back seat, bracing my hands on the top of the front seat, while Julie, Mary and my Mum laughed nervously. I couldn't believe it but we actually made it on time! I gave the cab driver a healthy tip and we ran in to catch our flight. What a day!

Things began moving fairly quickly, which was the start of the morale booster I needed. The scheduling nurse called to tell me I'd be admitted to the hospital the first week of March and be in the hospital for who knows how long? I needed to keep my weight up and eat a lot of calories because once I'm admitted I know I won't like the hospital food and will probably lose weight.

I scheduled an appointment with the Red Cross to have them collect two units of blood, which would be used as a backup in case I needed it during surgery. They refrigerated it and shipped it to the hospital. Now I was all set up with having my own blood in stock.

January 30, 2005. My admission was only a month and a week away. I wanted it to happen, but now that the date was actually scheduled I thought about it more and more every day and tried to keep busy. Nonetheless I was getting more nervous as the days were counting down. The schedule Dr. Man had planned was pretty aggressive, but exactly what they were going to do depended on what he saw once the surgeries began. An x-ray can only show so much, so it was either going to be worse or better than expected. My family and I had to schedule plane tickets and find lodging for whoever was going to fly out with me.

February 5, 2005. I haven't discussed the surgeries much with my family. There's no use in getting them more nervous than they already are. I decided the best way to explain the surgeries was to give them the high level points of what the doctor was going to do.

Telling my family about multiple surgeries is going to be stressful, especially when they are going to be dragged out over several weeks. I'm not nervous myself. I want to get on with it. I have been waiting for so long and now it is finally here. I recall the saying "be careful what you wish for" because I'm about to get it. I have to face facts, following surgery I might have serious post-operative complications…. SERIOUS COMPLICATIONS!

February 11, 2005. My family had many questions for Mary Jane, the scheduling nurse, before the first surgery. A teleconference call was scheduled. Family members were asked to write down their questions before the actual call, to minimize the amount of time the call would last. The majority of questions were about what I would be going through after each of the surgeries. For instance, she was asked to explain how the traction would work after the first surgery. Would I be in the orthopedic ICU the entire time after having my surgeries? The schedule nurse couldn't answer that with a definite answer as it would depend on me. If things were going well, would the doctor lessen the amount of time I would be in traction? The answer to that question was no. I would be in traction the entire time between the first and second surgeries- two weeks on my back. By the end of the call I think that my family had a little better understanding of what was going to take place. I had to stay focused and not get bogged down with all the details that Mary Jane shared. It could only add to my anxiety.

February 12, 2005. My family got together to discuss the upcoming events. Mum told us that she wanted to be in Cleveland the entire time I was there and Dad would be there the first week and then come back sometime later in the month for my second and third surgeries.

Peggy suggested that if it was possible, each sibling could come for a week and stay with Mum and Dad in Cleveland. This whole process would be very stressful for them, since they were in their late seventies and we wanted to minimize their stress.

Sue sent out a calendar for March and April through email to my brothers and sisters and they signed up for the weeks they could come to Cleveland. Each had to decide whether they would be flying or driving and make their arrangements. They also had to make arrangements regarding their jobs, the day to day care of their families while they were gone, what expenses they would incur while away from home, who could cover for appointments, and where they would stay while they were in Cleveland.

Someone had found out there was a place that families could stay while their family members were getting treatment at the clinic. It was called the Hope Lodge and was affiliated with the clinic. Generally, only family members could stay there that had to travel a long distance to support their family member, while they were receiving treatment. The price to stay there is relatively inexpensive. It is run by a non-profit organization and relies heavily on donations received, which is why the cost of staying is low. The lodge has a large kitchen stocked with dishes, pots and pans and anything else a person might need for cooking. The lodgers have to supply their own food and cook their own meals, which is nice because you can get tired of eating at the hospital all the time. And there are shuttle buses coming and going from the clinic back to the lodge at all times of the day and night, which was nice because not everyone was going to rent a car, if they flew in.

Two rooms were reserved at the Lodge for 14 – 20 days, depending on who was coming when. The only time they would be at the lodge is to sleep, eat, or shower; otherwise, they would be at the hospital with me. Additional reservations were made at a hotel to stay at after the 20 days.

There is a lot of coordination between businesses in the area and the Cleveland Clinic. The concierges at most hotels would contact the shuttle bus service on your behalf and setup the time the bus would pick you up each day. If you did rent a car you would have to get to the parking ramp by 8:00am to find a spot, otherwise, you would have to park quite a distance from the clinic. There are 10 different buildings within the clinic campus and each was for a different specialty. There are tunnels built underneath the buildings so patients can be moved from one building to another without having to go outside. This is great because Cleveland can have some huge snow storms in the winter.

Everyone's email addresses were confirmed and a master list was created and sent to everyone to be used while they are in Cleveland. Sue would find a computer in the hospital during the first week, which could be used to send out daily emails on my surgeries and progress. Communication is very important when you come from a large family.

It was great to see the teamwork they exhibited when designing the schedule and the communication plan. That teamwork provided me with the knowledge that my family would be there with me the entire time. I can't imagine someone coming for medical treatment to a place that was far away from their home and not having the support of family and friends. It could definitely affect their morale and healing process.

Chapter Thirty Three

Surgery Number One

March 5, 2005. Mum, Dad, Sue and I flew to Cleveland on Sunday and checked into the Hope Lodge. We arrived early afternoon and wanted to kill some time so we drove around Cleveland to see some of the city. We drove by the Rock and Roll Hall of Fame. Sue asked if I wanted to go through it and I said no. I had too much on my mind. My back has been in constant pain for three years and now this hopefully is going to change for the better.

March 6, 2005. Today I have my pre-op appointment with Dr. Man and Mary Jane. This was the first time that Dr. Man gave a more in-depth description of what the process would be for my surgeries. Mum, Dad, and Sue listened intently. Sue took notes, which she would share with the rest of the family.

During the first surgery Dr. Man would cut the sternum so that it would pop back into place, since it was cracked. Then he would take out two of my lower ribs that would be used for the second surgery. Dr. Man would turn me on my side and go to the part of my spine that had some ligaments wrapped around it and clip them. These ligaments were not allowing me to stand up straight and kept me hunched over. Then a halo would be put on my head with two screws in front and two screws in back. They would be screwed into my skull to hold the halo in place. The halo would have a rope attached at the top and it would be tied to the end of the bed. I would be put in a bed that had slippery sheets on it and the bed would be sloping downward with my feet lower than my head for two weeks. The gravity was supposed to stretch my spine, straighten it out, and give me some of my height back. The halo would be kept on until Dr. Man felt comfortable in moving on to my second surgery. During this time, I would be totally bedridden, so getting up to stretch my legs would be out of the question.

For the second surgery, Dr. Man will fuse my spine, using titanium rods to strengthen my back. The rods, which are sixteen inches in length, will be attached to my spine with screws and will run down from my lower thoracic through the lumbar region. The two ribs that have been removed will now be ground down into fine powder and sprinkled along both sides of the titanium rods. The Kyphoplasty cement material will be filled in where any vertebrae show signs of compression fractures or if tumors are detected in the spine, which is not uncommon with myeloma patients.

During the third procedure, the sternum will be reattached and supported with a titanium plate so there will be no chance of the bone breaking free. I know it sounds like a lot of work, and it is, but I don't have much choice if I want to see a significant improvement with my pain and posture. All this will take several weeks, but I'm not too disappointed about having to be in the hospital again for over six weeks. You have to remember, I was previously in the intensive care wing and quarantined for over two and a half months. I'm definitely nervous and apprehensive after listening to everything he has to say. The tension is a lot greater when he's explaining all this directly to me. It really hit me now - the reality of what's going to begin tomorrow.

Since this was such a dangerous process I think Dr. Man wanted everyone to be aware of exactly what was going to take place. He answered any questions we had and said that my most recent x-rays and MRI revealed that my bones were in good shape, which is what we were all hoping for. Good news to start the day off with. We had been with Dr. Man for about an hour and then I told Mum, Dad, and Sue that I wanted to speak with Dr. Man alone. They went out in the hall to wait.

I'd rehearsed this talk many times at home, and I only needed to say my piece and move on. I said to him "Doc I need you to go to the next level with this. I need you to be aggressive in your approach." He looked at me thoughtfully for a moment and replied, "I'm going to do the best that I can, do it safely and give you the best results." Yeah, stated like a cool cat. And for whatever reason I shook his hand and became teary-eyed and choked up. Normally I don't get too emotional, even through all this illness, but Dr. Man seemed to understand. He said he's encountered many people with myeloma and they go through a lot, so he understood my reaction. And just like that, we moved on, and everybody came back into the room. When my Dad saw that I was teary-eyed, he asked "Did you get some bad news?" I just shook my head and said "No."

While Mum, Dad, and Sue were out of the room, Mary Jane explained to them how the process works in the "P" surgery building and how often the family would receive updates. There is a huge electronic bulletin board in the waiting area and each patient is assigned a number. The number will be used the entire day to identify the patient, due to HIPPA requirements. For example, when a patient goes into the prep area the number will appear on the board with "Status of Prep". The statuses will be updated by nurses and Mary Jane as they change. If a patient has had a status for a long period of time, you could go up to the front desk and they would call the operating room to get a more up-to-date status and how long it would be before the next status change. Communication is so important for families to help keep their anxiety in check.

All the unknowns of the surgery are a gamble, which I am willing to take. I've thought about every problem that could arise following the surgeries – including the possibility that I could be paralyzed or even die. At this point, no new concerns are going to sway my decision; it's a go in my mind.

When all our questions were answered we left to have some dinner. We went back to the Lodge. I no longer felt nervous, just anxious to get on with it. I've waited three years for this process and I'm hoping the wait is worth it. As I lie down for bed, I realize everything is going to change in twelve hours. My health is either going to be better or worse. Since I couldn't eat or drink after midnight I ate right up until I went to bed. I had a sandwich, some french fries, and topped it off with a bowl of oatmeal, which I knew would fill my stomach up.

March 7, 2005. I'm a morning person, so getting up early isn't a problem for me. My Dad is even more of a morning person, so he was up before me, which never makes my Mum happy. She'd naturally wake up a little later if my Dad didn't make too much noise - but he almost always did. After I showered and shaved we went down to the lobby to wait for our rental car. I had to be at the clinic at 6:30am for admittance. At the hospital I'm the first person to check-in for the day's schedule of surgeries. The check-in here is a little different than at most hospitals.

There is a big electronic bulletin board to the left of the main desk with all the patients' names, type of surgery, and schedule for surgery, and my name is near the top of the list. The display includes the protocol the patient is following, so you can see the patient's progress moving through the surgery. When I checked in, they gave me a coaster with a built -in buzzer that they use to buzz you when they're ready to come out and admit you. Other hospitals have this type of check - in system and it works pretty slick. You can get most of your questions answered about where a patient is by looking at the screen. I sat down and we waited. My surgery is scheduled for 7:30am.

Soon a scheduling nurse showed me to a changing room where I could change into a gown. We went through the normal routine of getting my blood pressure, temperature, and pulse rate - all normal. After that the nurse left the small room, which was about the size of a normal bathroom. I was left alone. I watched a little TV while I waited for them to take me in. I'm getting SportCenter on TV, so my morning isn't a total loss. It takes my mind off getting ready for surgery. The nurse tells my family that my surgery would take about 5 hours and then I would be in the recovery room for about 2 more hours. The nurse also gave them the code they could use to identify my status on the big electronic bulletin board in the waiting area. It must have been forty-five minutes before they came in to get me and put me on a hospital gurney and wheeled me away. I didn't get a chance to talk with my family during this time because we were moving so fast from one hallway to another.

When I reached the area outside my operating room I noticed there was a wall clock that reminded me of the clocks you see in schools, the same simple design. On my right, across the hall, is a giant computer screen with a spreadsheet of all the surgeries scheduled for today. I'm the only patient out in the hall so far, since it's so early in the morning. Everyone else in this area is wearing hospital scrubs with hair nets and carrying on with their conversations as they walk by.

Time is creeping by, but it's not like I have anyplace better to be. Anyway, we aren't on my time, we are on the surgeon's time. Everybody walking by in their scrubs is talking like it's just another day for them, while I am lying out in the hall in a hospital gown covered with a blanket, waiting for my life to be forever altered. This is humorous.

It's chilly out here and the nurse put another blanket over me when I told her I could use one. I passed the time watching people go by and listening to the chatter. I occasionally looked at the clock. I couldn't have any reading material, because this was a sterile zone. An hour goes by. Now it's 8:30 and I'm starting to get antsy and uncomfortable lying on my back for so long. But there's nothing I can do about it; they'll get to me when they're good and ready. Finally, at about 9:15, they wheeled me into a big surgical station with all these surgical attendants moving about doing their thing. It's a slick set up. Imagine a round pie pan. In the middle is the giant room where they prep the patient, surrounded by a number of pie - shaped rooms. Each room is for a particular surgery for the day. Once that surgery is done, they start the whole process again with a new patient. My Dad finds out that on the day of my surgery there are one hundred surgeries scheduled!

It's cold in the room and the blanket that I have on is not doing the job. A nurse asks how I am feeling and tells me, "We're going to move you over to the surgical table. Do you need a hand?" I said "No, I can do it." They put on the mask that makes you sleepy, and then started to put those round patches on my upper body with wires attached. I do like the feeling of the drugs they gave to make me drowsy. I'm not feeling any pain in my body now. Man was I flying high, my body felt like it was floating and that's the last thing I remember about the surgery. I don't have a problem with anesthesia so I am out in a hurry. How do I know? I asked afterwards. They asked me a dozen times how I was feeling. Hey, if I wasn't feeling good about being here I would've given up a long time ago. There's no turning back now.

Sue said the waiting area was huge, about the size of a high school basketball court. Since my surgery was one of the first they were able to get a good seat on a comfortable sofa. Approximately 185 surgeries are performed in building "P" three days a week. They were told that updates would be given every hour. They notified my family of the time that surgery started. Updates were provided to them at 10:00am and 11:00am. By 11:00am all the sofas and chairs were full and eventually there was even people sitting on the floors. Since my family didn't want to lose their good seats they took turns walking around or getting something to eat.

The patient concierge came over to them and introduced himself and gave them some additional information about the clinic. He told them that the clinic had purchased the land in the area of the city that was really run down and was working on rejuvenating it. There were already ten new buildings and they are all connected, which is nice since they get lots of snow.

The 12:00 update was that things were going well. About 2:30 Mary Jane came to see the family and they immediately thought something was wrong. She told them that it took Dr. Man three hours to cut through the scar tissue to get to my spine and that would increase the amount of time for the entire surgery.

My family was concerned about the amount of time that I was under anesthesia and Mary Jane said they didn't need to worry, that I was doing fine. She said things were going according to plan with what Dr. Man wanted to accomplish. They continued to receive hourly updates. Finally around 5:30 the desk called my family up and said I was going to recovery, and that Dr. Man would be down shortly to talk to them. By this time almost the entire family waiting area was empty and there were approximately 150 people there during the day. I was one of the last patients out of surgery that day.

Dr. Man came down at 6:15pm and looked drained but excited. He told everyone he had done this type of process one other time and that mine was much more successful. I would go to recovery for a couple of hours and then be moved to ICU. He also said I am a strong person to be going through this. Sue said all 3 of them hugged and said how relieved they were I was in recovery. The entire surgery took nine hours. My family gathered all their stuff, got something to eat and then found the recovery room, which was in a different building. When they got there they found out that they were not going to allow the family in the recovery room so Mum and Dad went to the ICU.

All day long Sue had been calling family back home to give them updates. She setup a conference call for 10:00pm, for the entire family, so more details could be given.

When I woke up, it was dark in the recovery area. It's around nine o'clock at night, and the anesthesia was wearing off. Nobody's around, the place is quiet and empty, so I thought. The pain from the surgery appeared quickly. I don't even know if I could describe how bad it hurt. I had a remote attached to my hospital bed with the nurse's call button, and I buzzed her once I realized the morphine wasn't working to alleviate any of the pain. The nurse explained that I am on a morphine drip. I can press the button every fifteen minutes to help relieve the pain. I did that, but it wasn't helping with the pain. I told the nurse that the pain was unbearable and the morphine wasn't working. She gave me a shot of something stronger, which was supposed to last for four hours.

Sue stayed in the waiting area of the recovery room. She thought it was ridiculous that family was not able to see me. So she walked into the recovery room and proceeded to tell the nurse that we were from Wisconsin and that it would be beneficial for me to see a family member when I opened my eyes.

The nurse finally gave in and made Sue wear a mask and gown before entering recovery. Sue said there must have been 20 people in the recovery room, all hooked up to monitors. She was taken back when she saw me. She forgot about the halo being on and she said I looked like a robot being constructed. When she approached my bed she said I was moaning. She wanted me to know that family was there and she held my hand for awhile. When I went back into my drowsy stage she left to find Mum and Dad to prepare them for seeing me the first time.

The shot the recovery room nurse gave me only lasted for two hours and it began to wear off as soon as I was moved to the ICU. The pain was unbearable. When I was moved to the ICU Mum and Dad were shocked to see me with the halo on and all the additional wires and tubes that were attached to me. They could tell I was in a lot of pain. My family all thought how was I going to be able to be in this traction for two weeks?

The ICU was one huge room that was divided into 8 separate areas by curtains. The area was so small that only one person could stand next to the bed. The other two would have to stand out in the hall at the foot of the bed. You could hear other patients, their family members, their monitors, and all the other health care staff talking around you. When I was moved to the ICU a nurse came in right away and took my vitals. She explained to me where I was, what was going on and why I couldn't move my head.

About an hour later two x-ray technicians came into my room and said that they needed to take an x-ray of my back and that they would have to roll me on my side to slide the x-ray plates under me. Sue could see that I was in a lot of pain just lying in bed, and saw the look on my face when they said they would have to roll me. She told them that they would not be taking those x-rays tonight because of the pain I was in.

The technicians didn't know how to respond. She told them a second time that they would not be able to take the x-rays tonight. They said they would have to call the surgeon about this. After getting off the phone with the doctor they came back to my area and said that the x-rays would be taken at a different time and they left. This was a big relief for me. The nurse told me she needed to call Dr. Man to see if it was okay to give me another shot before the first shot's four hour time period ended.

Meanwhile, I started freaking out and became very nervous about being by myself with no one to complain to - or so I thought. I didn't realize it but my family stood at the foot of my bed for hours after the surgery, continually badgering the nursing staff about calling the doctor to get authorization for more pain medication. I sounded like a cry baby because that was the only way I could deal with the pain.

Sue left my room about 9:30 to charge her cell phone to be prepared for the 10:00pm conference call with the family back home. She found a waiting room that had four other people in it. One of those people was a little girl that would intermittently start crying. You could tell she was tired and the mother finally wised up and took her home. Everyone called into the conference call and Sue read the notes she had taken over the course of the day. They had additional questions but she could hear the relief in their voices when they heard that I was awake and that Dr. Man had given a message of success. The call lasted about 45 minutes and then Sue came back to my room.

I would moan out loud and even that didn't help much. I don't know how long it took for that nurse to come back, but finally she's there, saying my doctor approved another shot, but that was going to be it. Finally! It hurts so bad in my chest that I could hardly stand it. The second shot helped for a while but it wore off after a few hours. My family left the hospital about 11:30 to get some rest and they would be back in the morning around 8:00am to talk with Dr. Man and Mary Jane when they were doing their rounds. This became their daily routine.

Now, the nighttime nurse took off and I had no one to moan to about my pain. Nonetheless, I started moaning and kept it up all night. I know it sounds crazy but it was the only way I could deal with the pain and it helped to a point.

I kept looking at the clock: one o'clock, two o'clock, three o'clock, four o'clock, and five o'clock. Finally around 6:00am the pain started to wear off and a nurse showed up. They gave me another shot and I finally dozed off at about 6:30. Later I found out that the night nurse was a temporary, and a bad one at that. But I made it through the worst part of the pain, and I could handle it after that.

March 8, 2005. Dr. Man arrived early the next morning to see how I'm doing and check my condition. It turns out I'm doing par for the course and am moved to a more permanent room for the foreseeable future. My hospital bed is in the critical care area, but I'm not quarantined like I was before, so visitors don't have to wear plastic gowns or masks when they enter my room. Dr. Man says the surgery was successful in "stretching" out my spine. Now gravity was going to take over. The head of my bed was elevated to allow my body to naturally stretch. My head was in a halo to keep me from moving my spine at all. There were small weights attached to the halo and to the head of the bed to help stretch my spine. My sternum had been cut to allow my torso to return to where it was three years ago. I am now completely immobile and will be for the next two weeks while my spine slowly works its way back into place. My pain was tolerable with the help of the morphine drip. I don't like pain meds - never have, never will-so I wasn't using as much as I should, and the doctors and nurses confronted me about it.

When I admit to them that I don't like using pain meds, they assured me that this was the best regime of addressing the pain and that I should start to follow the prescribed treatment. Fine, I did as they asked and everyone was happy.

Meanwhile my roommate, whom I couldn't see behind the curtain that separated our room, didn't want to be there in the worst way. I could hear him yelling at his family, probably for getting him put in the hospital in the first place. He wasn't at all cooperative. The clinic staff was having a hard time getting him to keep his catheter in, because he took it out himself. I'm thinking that would hurt no matter how much you want it out. Listening to him rant and rave, I kept thinking this was no place for me, not in my condition. I wouldn't have a chance if this guy went crazy and decided to attack me just because I happen to be there. My family was thinking the same thing.

There is another reason why my family didn't want me staying in that particular area. Checking for cleanliness they found small puddles of yellow liquid underneath my bed. Evidently, the housekeeping staff hadn't done a very good job or they wouldn't have missed that. Considering my previous infections, this was a bad situation, especially when I just came out of surgery and my immune system was low to begin with. The family also discovered exposed wires that were probably connected to raising and lowering the bed. That was another safety hazard that needed to be addressed. It didn't take long for my family to get in touch with the hospital case manager and get me transferred to a different room. I don't know exactly what they said, but in a few hours I was moved into a new room on the secondary ICU floor. Good! I wasn't going to miss that guy at all. The case manager even told my family that this wasn't an episode that happened very often-if at all- at this clinic. I believed the case manager, after all, this clinic is world-renowned. This was just an instance where somebody slipped up.

To kill some time today, Sue went on a hunt for a computer that she could use to send out daily updates to the rest of the family. She located one a couple of floors below my room and sent out her first update. This became another daily ritual.

March 9, 2005. Dr. Man came in between two surgeries and made some small talk with me. Then he turned to my Mum and asked if she noticed anything different about me. Mum had a puzzled look on her face and the doctor said to look at my profile. My chin was above my shoulders, which wasn't the case for at least a couple of years. They also noticed that I looked taller lying in bed. We all got tears in our eyes due to the realization that the surgery had worked.

I was still in a lot of pain the second, third, and fourth days after surgery. All my family could do for me was to give me ice chips or ice water when I was thirsty. Dad was going stir crazy from having to sit for long periods of time, so he would get up and take long walks around the hospital. I would look at Mum and Sue and roll my eyes. That was one thing I could do while lying there. Another thing I could do while laying there was to listen to someone read me the sports section of the newspaper. Dad would always make sure that we had a newspaper each morning to read. This was a normal thing we would do every day at home and it helped to bring some normalcy to my days in the ICU.

There were some real crazy patients in the secondary ICU. One man, who was about seventy-five years old, kept trying to take his gown off. He was on a lot of medications. The staff tied his hands to the sides of the bed, but he always managed to get out of the straps. He started to take his gown off, and tried to get out of bed. Mum and Sue would look at each other and start to laugh. It was comical to watch the staff hustle to put his gown back on before he was completely naked.

Tomorrow, Tomas will be flying in and Sue and Dad will be flying home. Dad will be able to work off some of his energy and not feel like a caged animal. It will be good to see a new face and have someone else to talk to. I can always talk sports with Tomas, so we will have a lot of catching up to do. March is the time of the year for the college men's basketball tournament –March Madness - so to keep my sanity I picked the teams I felt would win their games. Sue marked them on the newspaper listings and taped the paper to the wall on the right side of my bed. I had picked the last two tournament winners for both Sue and her husband's office pools. She must have spread the word to the staff about my successes and I began to have foot traffic in my room from all sorts of clinic employees, ranging from Dr. Man's personal secretary to clinic nurses, wanting to look at my choices. It broke up the monotony of lying on my back for two weeks, so I didn't mind the company. It gave me something different to talk about other than the normal questions, like "How are you doing?" or "How are you feeling today?"

There was a patient who was a minister in one of the curtained areas of the ICU and he was getting quite a bit of attention from the nursing staff. Mum was getting pissed that they weren't paying more attention to me. But the staff probably thought that since I had family there that they would take care of getting me anything I needed.

The nurses wanted me to start eating something to get my bowels moving since I had been immobile, so they brought in some applesauce and wanted me to start drinking more water. Since I wasn't able to move from side to side Mum, Dad, or Sue would have to feed me and give me drinks. After I started eating fruit I was able to take a healthy shit and then I felt a little better.

March 10, 2005. Today, Sue and Dad were flying home. That was a good thing because Dad was going stir crazy while sitting in my room, which was unnerving for Mum. She understands that Dad needs to be on the go all the time doing something. Tomas was coming today and his flight would arrive about an hour and a half before Sue and Dad left.

Sue took Mum downstairs to show her where the computer was for Tomas to use in sending out daily updates to the family back home and she gave Mum the email master list. Mum went to the airport to meet Tomas and say goodbye to Dad and Sue. When Tomas arrived they had about a half hour to visit before they had to board their plane. Tomas was going to stay four or five days. Mum and Tomas took a shuttle back to the hospital.

When Tomas saw me for the first time with my halo on he was surprised. You can only imagine what a person looks like when they say they have a halo on, but when you actually see the person it is a different story. It was good to catch up with Tomas and we started to talk about sports. He saw my March Madness basketball tournament picks on the wall and we spent hours analyzing them. That's what we usually did before any tournaments began. It was good to have someone here that was as interested in sports as I am. It took my mind off my medical issues for short periods of time. Tomas was good at knowing when I wanted to talk and when I didn't.

March 15, 2005. The time that Tomas was with me flew by and before I knew it he was flying home. Mary flew in from Madison and Steve flew in from Portland, Oregon to stay with Mum for a week. I couldn't move much, not that I didn't try, but two weeks seemed like a long time to just lie. The screws in both sides of my forehead and in the back of my head were pressing just enough to drive me crazy.

If I had an itch on my head, I'd try to scratch it. If I couldn't reach it, I would get someone in the family to scratch it. Mum said that the itching was being caused by the healing taking place around the screws. After a few days, Mary bought me a small back scratcher, in case I needed to scratch and nobody was around. Thanks again Mary!

Mary, Mum, and I talked with Steve about when they started investigating this type of surgery and the path everyone had gone down to find out about Dr. Man and the Cleveland Clinic. Their persistence brought me to this point and I was so grateful. It's all about family and hard work.

On the last day of Mary and Steve's stay, Peggy arrived with her husband Dan and daughters. They would be here for my second surgery. It was hard to have Mary and Steve leave. I didn't know when the next time would be when I would see Steve since he lived in Oregon. And Mary always brings a smile to my face.

Chapter Thirty Four

Surgery Number Two

Before proceeding with the second operation, the ribs taken out during the first surgery had to be biopsied to make sure they were not diseased and therefore useless for my second surgery. When the pathology report on the ribs came back, it was all good news - no myeloma or tumors. Yeah baby, yeah! The myeloma seemed to be under control. Everybody was relieved.

As the week went on I looked forward to watching the basketball tournament games with my family. I hadn't had any complications arise from the first surgery. As of right now the second surgery was a go. This was going to be the most dangerous of all the procedures that I was scheduled to have. Dr. Man was going to place the rods and screws in my back, and I would be lying face down on the operating table the entire operation. Any surgery you have can lead to complications and you have to make yourself aware of all the possibilities. I knew the risks going in, the surgeon had sat down and explained them to me and I am as prepared for what could happen as I was ever going to be.

March 21, 2005. I slept well the night before surgery. I usually don't get too nervous, even for something like this. I just wanted to get on with it. I had waited three years for my back to feel better. The day of the second surgery I was a little more apprehensive because of the seriousness of the surgery but we were going to get on with it. The thoughts running through my head about what could go wrong was making me nervous.

The precision with which it would take to do this procedure and the chances to make a mistake were two of my biggest concerns. One slip up with a cut and I could be paralyzed for the rest of my life. Would my lungs be able to handle it through the procedure? What if there were complications and the team had to stop before the procedure was completed? You get where I'm coming from? I was thinking about anything and everything that could go wrong. It only took me three seconds counting backwards from one hundred and I was out from the anesthesia. How do I know that? I asked the staff afterwards.

At 4:55 pm my family was called to meet with Dr. Man in the conference room. He was excited about the progress made today and showed off two comparative x-rays, one before surgery and one after. The difference was amazing, and he was "ecstatic" about the results. I had gained 3 inches. My neck and head were squarely on my shoulders, supported by a spinal column, which now had titanium hardware. The halo was off. A breathing tube was put in to ensure my breathing was ok and I would be in the recovery room overnight. The breathing tube would be taken out tomorrow if everything went ok. It was likely that I would be going to the H building tomorrow, which is a recovery building for spinal surgery patients. Peg sent an end-of-surgery e-mail update to everyone back home.

The next thing I remember was waking up in a dark room and no one was around. I was lying in a bed in a recliner position. The first thing I did was wiggle my toes to see if I could still move them. Whooa! Was I relieved when I could wiggle all my toes and move my legs. A nurse came in shortly after this and asked how I was feeling and I said "I feel fine now".

My sister Peg came in the room and was smiling and said "you did great". She asked how I was doing I said "I'm fine". I ask her what time it was and she said 8:30pm. I asked her how long I was in surgery, and she said it was about eight hours. She told me all the specifics of the surgery, but I was so out of it from the anesthesia that I was too tired to care. I was beat; I didn't have any energy left. Judging by her reaction, everything came out alright in the end. I made it, I made it thru! YYYYYEEEEESSSSSSSSSSS!

Peg filled me in on what transpired during the surgery after I was fully awake. She said they had taken those two rib bones they had been storing and used them successfully. There was more scar tissue than Dr. Man had anticipated and it took longer than expected to remove it.

Dr. Man filled in tumors he found in my bones with the cement like substance that was used in my Kyphoplasty surgeries. One of my lungs was "deflated" so they could reach an area of my spine. The titanium rods were inserted in my back and the ground rib bones were sprinkled on both sides of my spine to allow a strong attachment from the bones to the metal. Since I was lying on my stomach through the whole procedure, they had placed my head in a form fitting, styrofoam head gear to keep my head in the right position the whole surgery. I don't know when it happened but my lung wouldn't inflate and start working again like it was suppose to. That is when they put in a breathing tube. I didn't feel anything during the whole procedure. I didn't have any dreams or see any lights; I was completely out of it – thank God! I'm on my back and I had a fair amount of pain the next two days, but it would be nowhere near as severe as it was after the first surgery.

March 22, 2005. Dr. Man was going to go ahead with the third surgery for the sternum. But I had lost two-and-a-half liters of blood and they usually stop surgery at two liters lost. So he thinks that this next surgery would be scheduled for the following week. Dr. Man said I would be sore for the next few days. The halo was off! The incision in my back is about 18 inches long.

The night nurse came in at 8:00 pm and gave me my shot of fentanol. I would be getting an additional shot of pain medication at midnight and at 8:00am. I continued to use my "pain pump," every 15 minutes. Dr. Man's colleague stopped by and indicated that they think I would be moved to H62 tomorrow if I am able. That is where I started out before surgery.

I'm allowed visitors for five minutes in the next one and a half hours and only two visitors at a time. Dr. Man was looking for blood donations from my family to have ahead of time for my next surgery, just to be safe. He had already used up the blood that I gave at the Red Cross and was shipped to the hospital. I hoped this was not going to be a problem. My family knew my blood type so we'd see if any of them were a match. I'd rather not use someone's blood outside of my family for safety concerns. All in all, Dr. Man was happy with the outcome. I don't know why but the second surgery hadn't left me in more pain and discomfort. I cannot explain it, but I am glad that's the way it had worked out.

March 24, 2005. Today Peg and her family were heading home. It's always hard when family is leaving and I am still here. I am so grateful though that they were able to come and provide support. Dad came back today and Tricia, Julie, and Kirsten would be arriving on Thursday or Friday and staying through the weekend, which was Easter.

Day two of recovery Dr. Man wanted me to sit up in a wheelchair for half an hour. The hardest part was getting out of bed to get into the wheelchair. I had to be coached in the proper way to do it. It took me a number of times before I got the hang of this way of getting out of bed because I was unsure of the pain that would accompany this movement. I wasn't confident in doing this the first few times and the nurses had to help me get over my fear. Who would have ever thought it would take me several minutes just to roll out of bed? But it did. I finally managed to sit up at the side of the bed with the help of the nurse.

Dr. Man wanted me to sit up for a few minutes and then stand up with the help of two nurses, helping me balance myself. I knew it was going to hurt at first so I prepared for it. I cautiously stood up with the nurses lifting me under my arm on either side. It was a struggle but I made it.

My Mum and Dad were in my room when I sat up on the side of the bed. My Mum excused herself to go out into the hall, because she was crying from the emotion of seeing me stand up for the first time in three weeks. It takes a lot before my Mum shows her emotions. In fact, I don't ever recall seeing her get emotional in front of me. She just doesn't. I guess it was a powerful moment. My Dad stayed in the room to lend a hand in getting me off the edge of the bed into the wheelchair.

My whole body didn't feel as bad when I sat up as I thought it was going to. My back felt stiff more than actually painful. I was relieved I was able to sit up, but I was cautious in how my body was adjusting to having all this surgery and a reconstructed back. I didn't feel dizzy at all. This was the first time in three weeks that I had sat up.

There was one problem that developed post-surgery. My chin became irritated and had developed an infection from being in the foam support for over eight hours during the second surgery. My Mum brought up the fact that my chin was discolored. I hadn't looked in the mirror to see what it looked like. My chin turned purple and it was very sensitive when it was touched. The head nurse and my Mum were the only ones who could wash it without causing considerable pain. I couldn't shave at all, so we just trimmed the whiskers on my chin.

March 26, 2005. Tricia, Julie, and Kirsten arrived today. It was good to see them and I knew Mum was happy some girls were here. They were so happy to see me stand up straight. They had to feel a great sense of accomplishment in seeing how I looked now. Tricia and Julie's persistence, in finding Dr. Man and the Cleveland Clinic, contributed to my success in straightening my spine and alleviating my back pain.

It wasn't until a week after the second surgery that the infectious disease doctor addressed the chin problem. When a part of your body is discolored and sensitive after surgery, you should address it before a week goes by. At first the specialist, who looked at my chin, didn't want to say what the problem was, but my Mum knew it was MRSA. Yah, I'm pissed off.

Nobody in the hospital wanted to admit it, but that's what it was. The solution was to put on a cream three times a day to keep the area moist and get the area to form a scab. The problem was a new layer of skin would be forming under the layer of cream and my chin was very sensitive to touch. The skin specialist explained that it would be months before a new layer of skin would replace the damaged skin.

Besides my Mum, there was only one nurse who I trusted to administer the cream, without creating too much pain, and when that nurse went on vacation, I only allowed Mum to take care of this. Nobody in the clinic was too concerned that my infection was bacterial, because they didn't quarantine me from any of the clinic staff or prevent me from having a roommate.

The other complication I encountered after surgery was a damaged vocal cord. The anesthesiologist had to stick a breathing tube down my throat during the second surgery, and unfortunately it damaged my left vocal cord, so I couldn't speak above a whisper. Nobody knew whether it would heal with time or be damaged for good. Dr. Man scheduled an appointment to have a throat specialist stop by my room to see what could be done to remedy the vocal cord issue. This was a week after surgery, the same time the chin infection was addressed. They were even talking about possibly having surgery if my throat didn't improve. To check out my vocal cords, the throat specialist used a tube with a viewing device. The problem was that the tube went through my nose deep into my throat and hurt like hell! His exam confirmed that my left vocal cord was damaged - to what extent, he couldn't say for sure.

We would schedule an appointment to see an ear, nose, and throat specialist once we got home. Yeah, I am worried about how much damage there was and if anything could be done about the fact that I couldn't speak above a whisper.

Tricia and Julie felt it would be better to write things down versus trying to speak, so they got a pad and pencil for me to use. I never thought that I would be communicating this way again. It was good for Mum to have them here since Dad would become anxious and want to be on the go again. This time though I was able to move around more and be more active with Dad.

Mum and the girls found the chapel in the clinic and went to have some quiet time. Mum always draws on her faith to get through tough times. She was probably very thankful though when praying now. Her son had come through two serious surgeries without major complications.

The girls left on Easter and I hoped it would not be long before I would be going home too. Two surgeries were done, hopefully only one more to go. I hadn't been told yet what the plan was, but I sensed I was in the home stretch. I was holding up pretty well. My vital numbers were stable and I hadn't developed any infections following the second surgery, other than the one on my chin.

Chapter Thirty Five

Surgery Number Three

The third surgery entailed Dr. Man putting my sternum back together. It had been three weeks since the sternum was left unattached, so that the first two operations could go as planned. Dr. Man had sawed apart my sternum and it was sitting on top of my lungs, so he could perform the other procedures. The need for a fractured sternum no longer existed, so Dr. Man was going to fuse the sternum back together and support it with a small titanium plate.

I was surprised he wasn't going to let it heal naturally and I asked him whether putting a plate in was really necessary, I'm not happy about having still another surgery. Who would be? He explained that he wasn't confident that the sternum healing by itself would be strong enough. He felt it might collapse in the future, and he didn't want that to happen if he could help it. I wasn't going to win the argument, so I let it be. His mind was made up.

This surgery, from what Dr. Man said, would be the easiest from what he described to me the day of surgery. I just hope I could make it through surgery without complications. I still didn't know if this was the last surgery.

March 31, 2005. Here I am waiting in the hallway on the gurney for my third surgery at the end of March. I was hoping everything was going to be alright. Dr. Man came in when I was in the recovery room and explained that his surgical team had done multiple procedures and there would be no need to have any more surgeries. I was in and out of surgery in a few hours and everything went well. Done! Done! Done! I was so relieved that it was all over. So were Mum and Dad.

I was assigned to a room with a patient who just had the same surgery I did, but with a different doctor. He was a nice guy. If I would have had a choice though, I would have had a private room. Available beds were scarce at the clinic. The room was the size of a dorm room and a curtain separated his side of the room from mine.

My roommate was a little too confident in his abilities, because the second night in our room he got out of bed without assistance of a nurse, stumbled in his corner of the room and got a big cut in the side of his head. I heard him fall but I didn't see it happen because the curtain separated us.

I'm glad I missed seeing that; I didn't need to relive that every day. As a result, his doctor decided that he was going to be transferred out of the room and put on a twenty- four- hour lockdown, because he was a danger to himself. Personally, I thought this decision was a little extreme, but who am I to say? I am sure of one thing. I wasn't going to go for a walk without someone being alongside me, in case I stumbled. I could get up and move around in the room using my walker, but this was as far as I would venture without someone by my side. It wasn't that I was afraid of falling. I just didn't need to have a setback in my recovery from falling, when I could have prevented it.

My Dad was the one who walked the halls with me. I usually walked three times a day for about half an hour each time. It was early spring and the weather was getting nice, so we decided to go outside and get some fresh air. I hadn't been outside for over three weeks. It was too far for me to walk with a walker from my room down to the front entrance, so Dad wheeled me down in a wheelchair. The fresh air felt so good, and the cool breeze was worth the trip. I either read or just sat outside and watched the world go by. My Dad would bring his Louis L'Amour western paperback books along to read, and he dived into one whenever he had the chance.

I started rehab right away after the third surgery. Naturally, my therapist was with me for my first appointments. We worked on easy movement and finding out where my starting point was for reference. I picked up on the exercises pretty quickly. After a few appointments my body was adjusting to the changes. I had a new roommate after being solo in my room for a few days. He just had his right shoulder operated on, and his arm was elevated in an uncomfortable looking way. I knew he was in a lot of pain because he asked for pain medication all the time. Boy, I knew how he felt; I was in that spot a month ago.

I was having a problem getting to sleep. My roommate didn't like me having my TV volume turned up high enough for him to hear, so I accommodated his request and kept it down. Ordinarily, I don't get a lot of sleep at night when I'm in the hospital, but most people never do. Three or four hours of sleep a night was all I was getting but it didn't seem to bother me too much. Having the TV on helped me sleep. I knew whenever I was discharged that I would catch up on my sleep.

After a few days with the second roommate I was moved to another room in a different wing of the clinic. My new roommate was an older gentleman from Ohio, who came to the clinic for a genetic heart condition. His family was very likable and an easy going group. His son handled a lot of the family's day- to- day decisions regarding his father's care. I could hear him discussing medical treatment with his father and mother together. I only had two complaints with the father. The first was he liked to have the room super warm at night, with the thermostat set at least at 78 degrees. I couldn't sleep when it was that warm in the room, so we would go back and forth, setting the thermostat up and down at night. If I turned it down to 70 degrees, it would somehow be turned up while I was out of the room. We finally came to a compromise in setting the thermostat at 72 to 74 degrees to satisfy him, his family, and myself.

The other complaint I had was that he was a real hacker (cougher) at bedtime. I don't think he realized he was doing it so much at night, but he would fall asleep and keep coughing. He was not the best roommate for someone who wanted to keep away from as many germs as possible. He would be sleeping like a baby in the morning and I would wake up at 6:00am.

Once I woke up, I would be up for the day. I would get up and go down to the lounge, using the walker to balance me. Nobody would be up yet, so it was quiet for at least a little while. I would watch TV and read the local paper until my breakfast tray was brought in either by the staff or most likely my Mum and Dad. I would eat the hospital food so I could get out of the hospital quicker, not because I liked it. My Mum, God love her, pushed the vegetables every day, especially beets. I hate them but I knew what she was getting at by ordering them, so I'd eat them. Dad would go wherever I wanted to go when I wanted to walk. Naturally, he had a happy attitude when he saw me making progress in rehab. My balance was getting better day by day.

I was only in the room a few days when I learned that my roommate's wife had taken a fall on a rubber mat at the clinic's entrance door. When she tripped, she braced her fall by extending her hands and ended up breaking her right hand and spraining her left hand. A few days after that I heard their son discussing her injuries with both parents. I guess the clinic felt responsible, because they already had made her a financial settlement offer, and the family was discussing whether to settle or not. There's always someone who's having a worse day than you are.

I had already been walking in the hallway for a week with the help of my Dad. I still needed help getting in and out of bed, which I hated. My two-and-a-half-year-old nephew had more freedom to move around than I did. This is where patience is needed in order to not take a step back in my recovery. I definitely didn't want that to happen.

Dr. Man never had a discussion with me about adjusting my pain medication. I assumed he had a plan. I just didn't think he'd be moving so quick on the adjustment. Right after my third surgery, he took me off the morphine drip completely. Just like that-cold turkey. I wasn't sure I would be able to handle it but surprisingly my body adjusted very well. If I did need help with the pain the nurses would give me an ibuprofen or two. It didn't help much so I didn't use it much after the first few times. I felt surprised and lucky at how quickly my body adjusted to the surgery and lack of medication. It didn't always work that easy. I guess all my exercising and eating right was paying off.

My physical therapy sessions were on the first floor. I needed to get my confidence back in using my back like it was supposed to be used in turning, bending, extending, and supporting my body. Naturally, I was babying my back and moving more cautiously until I became confident with it again. After only three days of therapy I felt that I had all the exercises I needed to keep me busy for awhile. Evidently, Dr. Man felt the same way, because in a surprise move he said he was going to release me in a few days. I was thinking that I'd be here for at least another week, but I guess that he felt I was well enough and focused enough on my rehab that I could fly home. My chin was still healing but the infection had been reduced with the ointment being used.

I was told by the nursing staff that I would be released April 7th. I was ecstatic and felt lucky coming through all the surgeries and rehab with only the chin issue and the vocal cord damage. The surgeries were finished and I made it!!

My parents were jumping up and down for joy. They had lived out of a suitcase for over a month and were cooped up in a hospital. That was very difficult for them because they were never gone from home that long before and like being outside. It just goes to show what sacrifices parents will make for their children. We all were looking forward to getting back home. The departure flight was confirmed and everything was set. All that was left to do was to see Dr. Man before my release.

April 7, 2005. Dr. Man checked my rehab progress and scheduled the first of many follow-up appointments I needed with him. Some small talk was made and then we shook hands and said our goodbyes to him and his assistant, Mary Jane. She did a great job in answering all the questions my family had before, during, and after the surgeries. About my surgeon, what can I say? He is "the Superman of spinal surgeons." All you have to do is research his background to get an indication of how much experience he has with extreme spinal procedures. He must have had a great feeling of satisfaction for what he accomplished during my surgeries and what he could physically see he had corrected in me. He truly went above and beyond my expectations and I am so grateful! It will be interesting to see what the medical staff back home think when they see me the next time.

The pain, besides following the first surgery, was relatively mild considering the number of surgeries and the severity of those surgeries. Pain has a funny way of playing with people's minds. Some patients can handle it better than others. Luckily, for whatever reason, I didn't have too much problem with the pain.

Chapter Thirty Six

Going Home

I was officially discharged now and running on time for our flight back home, but I was concerned about going through the security scanner. I didn't know if I would set the alarm off with this metal in my body. I suppose I could have shown them all my incisions. I walked up to the scanners, held my breath, and walked through. Nothing happened, no alarms went off. What a relief! We could make our flight on time and get back home by early evening.

By the time our flight landed the sun was going down, but it was a great springtime evening sunset. This was the perfect way to come back to my home state. Our house is out in the country and has a long gravel driveway behind some woods, so you couldn't see the driveway until you cleared the woods. Once we made it to the driveway, I saw all these balloons decorating the trees and all my nieces and nephews running around outside. They all came to greet us as we drove in. A welcome home party for sure, but it also happened to be my birthday. Not a bad birthday present. What a great surprise! I think Dr. Man knew when my birthday was, or else somebody told him. Either way, if it was possible, he was going to try and get me home for my birthday.

It was great to be in familiar settings and sleep in my own bed and not have a roommate. I could catch up on my sleep and start my rehab at the local hospital. I was anxious to get started. The food at home is way better than the hospital food, and I can work on gaining some weight back and gaining back strength as well. I started to get into a daily routine after only a few days back when I developed an infection in my lungs. Was it a result of the surgery?

Was it pneumonia? Three days after I was home, the home health nurse stopped in to check my vital signs, my breathing efficiency and chin. The pulse ox was checked by putting a snap on any finger and before long a number came up in red on the portable machine. My resting pulse ox was 91 percent oxygen efficiency and 87 percent when I was walking, which are both low. Based on these results, the nurse suggested I should be admitted to the local hospital. I couldn't believe this was happening. Sue and my Dad took me in to be admitted. I didn't think I would be back in a hospital this fast after coming home.

April 11, 2005. Dr. Lowe ordered a few basic tests such as a throat culture and chest x-ray. The x-ray showed I had fluid below my lungs, which is more serious than your typical cold. He started me on two antibiotics today. I had a temperature tonight of 99.5 degrees.

April 12, 2005. Dr. Lowe is all over this infection today, ordering several more tests, including a CAT- scan. The nurse indicates the initial diagnosis is pneumonia. My temperature was lower today than when I initially went into the hospital. An infectious disease doctor stopped in to look at my chin and find out what kind of infection I have. Is it MRSA or some other type of staph infection? Hopefully this doctor can clear things up. Dr. Lowe believed that the fluid buildup under my lungs was not pneumonia related. He appeared frustrated by these developments as there seemed to be a pattern here, i.e., the right vocal cord was paralyzed, and the area outside the right lung was generating fluid and pushing on my lower lobe.

Dr. Lowe consulted with several physicians, specifically a cardiac thoracic surgeon and a pulmonologist. I suggested Dr. Lowe speak with Dr. Man to discuss the fluid build- up and see if he had dealt with this before. Was there something that happened during one of the surgeries that could have caused this? Could Dr. Man share with Dr. Lowe any experiences he dealt with like this before and what the cause of it could be and what possible treatments there were? After the two doctors spoke, Dr. Lowe cultured the fluid and discovered it was a chyle fluid, pronounced "kyle" fluid for short, a white milky fluid that had built up outside the lungs, as a result of complications from surgery. The chyle fluid is responsible for the digestion of food.

Specifically, the thoracic duct had been interrupted or severed. Nobody was sure if fluid would continue to build up and become chronic or if it would go away. The only way to get the fluid out is to stick a needle in the lower right side of my back, under my lungs, and drain it out. Usually this complication occurs a few days after surgery, not ten or twenty days later. We were hoping the problem would be remedied by draining the fluid, after which the damaged area would heal itself. Otherwise they might have to repair it surgically. I didn't want to hear any more talk about surgery, especially with my back. I'm praying it wouldn't come to that, but time would tell. Dr. Lowe's colleague "Dr. Doom and Gloom" had another opinion. He told Dr. Lowe "You shouldn't have released him for the surgery." He believed, from my previous medical history, that the surgeries were too much of a risk for me. What did he know? He's not me and wasn't living with my skeletal condition. He also felt that Dr. Lowe should not treat me for the thoracic issue because it was a result of a surgery that was done at a different hospital.

He said since nobody on staff has ever seen this type of case that Dr. Lowe should excuse himself from my care and we should get somebody with more background in treating similar cases. The problem is that nobody in the area has ever seen a case like mine so we'd probably have to travel several hours away to find a doctor who had experience with anything similar to my case.

Knowing Dr. Lowe, he listened to his colleagues' advice but decided, nonetheless, to stay on my case. You only learn from a case like this by being involved with it, and that's what he decided to do. He had been in communication with my surgeon before and after my surgery, so they were on the same page regarding my care. I was thankful for that. I only learned about this conversation recently, so it was news to me too. I was always the last to find out about these meetings.

April 13, 2005. Dr. Lowe scheduled the drainage procedure. This procedure was going to hurt according to Dr. Lowe. Sticking a needle below my lungs does not sound good. They gave me a shot to numb the area where they were going to insert the needle. I was sitting up on an exam table while the nurse inserted the needle, and the numbing shot did not dull the pain. The nurse didn't get the needle inserted in the right spot the first time so she had to pull it out and reinsert it. When the needle was in the right spot the nurse could see the fluid draining out through the tube. Thank God! The nurse asked me if I wanted to see it draining out. I said "um no". The nurse, who put the tube in, left a memorable impression on me. She was called away while the needle was still inserted in my back. I guess the call must have been important, because I sat on that table for a long ass time, so angry I couldn't think straight, in so much pain from having the needle stuck in my back, and sitting there on the exam table waiting, waiting, and ... waiting.

Where was that dumb ass nurse? Any idiot knows you don't leave a patient during a procedure like that. The technician who was watching the procedure even had to page her to get her back into the room. The whole procedure should have taken about twenty minutes. Instead it took forty- five minutes of sitting up the whole time with my back getting really sore. I just had back surgery but somehow that slipped the staff's mind.

April 15, 2005. The fluid below my lungs returned two days later and they had to perform another procedure to drain the area. This time the procedure didn't take as long because the nurse didn't leave the room. The fluid amount was about six hundred cc's, compared to one liter the last time.

The next day Dr. Lowe decided that he would have the clear tube reinserted into my back and leave the tube in there for a period of time, in hopes that it would do the trick. I didn't have anything to lose at this point. I would be hooked up to this tube twenty- four hours a day. I went back down to the first floor to get the needle inserted with the tube attached. The fluid would drain into a plastic bag hanging on a stand to the right of my bed. Getting the needle inserted this time went a lot better. Obviously I would have to be careful how I moved, but I could still get around even with the tube attached. I just had to be careful not to yank the hose out by forgetting that it was there. I was worried about lying on the tube when I was in bed. But I didn't think it would be hard to remember it was there.

How long would I be a guest in the hospital? Dr. Lowe couldn't say; a week, maybe two. We would have to see. I became accustomed to having the tube in after a few days, not that I had a choice. I was just hoping, praying this would work. The next plan would be more severe. After day five the flow of fluid was decreasing, which was a good sign. It was also changing from a thicker, milky fluid to a clearer fluid. The infection was decreasing and the antibiotics were working. Dr. Lowe was hoping that once the tube was out everything would be all right.

My family was back taking turns staying with me, specifically my five sisters. I had a picc line in for all the antibiotics I was taking and a clear line in the right side of my lower back. I couldn't do any walking outside the room now, so all I could do was stand up and stretch my legs and walk in place. The family made sure I had newspapers and books to read.

I didn't think I would be in this type of situation again after being at Cleveland. Today, I had the same male nurse I had when I was in the hospital on the fifth floor. His name is Dave. I remember him because he is an athlete, who is into running and he'd talk about his daily jogs to work. We hit it off and he remembered me from my previous admissions to the hospital. It is always good to be able to talk to another athlete.

April 22, 2005. By day seven I was getting antsy to have this tube taken out. But Dr. Lowe wanted to be cautious and "observe" me for a couple more days- meaning at least three. Finally, on day nine, Dr. Lowe gave me the good news that I would be getting the tube taken out tomorrow and then be released. The treatment had worked. The leaked duct had resealed. I felt so relieved. I am so glad that Dr. Lowe was open minded enough to try new things and I have been able to benefit from his open mindedness.

April 30, 2005. My voice still sounded hoarse but I could speak a little clearer and I was easier to understand for the first time in a month. My throat was still very sore and so we went ahead and scheduled an appointment with a throat specialist. I am anxious to hear what the specialist had to say.

When I met the doctor he said he needed to use a device, with a tiny camera, which he would stick up my nose to allow him to look inside my throat. I could tell by the description of the procedure that it was going to hurt. The camera allows him to look on a TV screen and show me what he's seeing. He said he could tell the left vocal cord was still sore. How would this heal? Only time would tell. I would just have to wait and see.

The staph infection on my chin was conclusively MRSA and Dr. Lowe was not worried about it at this point. My chin scab covered my whole chin area, but I was glad it was starting to heal.

I wanted to get started as soon as possible with my physical therapy rehab for my back. I am walking with a couple of canes now instead of using the walker. Good riddance to it. I could finally walk outside by myself after three weeks of being home. I either walked early in the morning on our country road or later in the day in our orchard wearing my headphones. When I walked on the road, sometimes I would walk out of my parents' view and they would come driving down the road to see if something happened to me. What am I going to say? They were worried I might have fallen. Understandable, I was still pretty frail at this point. The more I walked, the better my appetite was. I needed to gain some weight back.

My physical therapy would be done at the hospital where I first was diagnosed. Someone has to drive me because I'm still not strong or confident enough to handle getting in and out of a vehicle or driving. I was getting closer, though. I will be happy when I can start driving again. My rehab is going well, though sometimes it feels like I'm not making a whole lot of progress. Some days I notice a big gain in my back's response to exercises and some days it's harder to see any change. I will get it though, I'm not a quitter. I will be better than ever when I get the right exercises that work for my back.

In between going to rehab I flew back to have post surgery check-ups with Dr. Man. I would fly with whoever, in my family, had the time to make the trip with me. If it was up to me, I would fly alone, but I wouldn't win that argument.

The trip I remember the most was when my brother Scott went with me. My appointment was on Monday morning and we flew in Saturday afternoon because the flights were cheaper then. So we had a day to go sightseeing if we wanted. But there was a "lake effect" snow storm, and the streets were full of snow and our rental car was buried in the parking lot under 8 inches of the white stuff. We didn't know this area so I was not too keen on going. Scott wanted to check out the sights but I said "no thanks."

My check-up was at two separate clinics. Don't ask me why. One appointment was out in the suburbs at the "satellite" clinic, 45 minutes from the main campus. The clinic was smaller than the main campus buildings. Still, it was larger than most clinics I was familiar with back home. It had three floors and a nice atrium as you walked in the entrance. The closest reasonably-priced hotel was 30 minutes away. So we got up early to follow the map directions, which could sometimes be less than reliable. Scott was driving, naturally- he wouldn't let me drive if his life depended on it- and I was in charge of directions. We made it on time, which was all that mattered.

I checked in at the front desk and we went up to the third floor to get x-rays of my back. It turned out they didn't have me scheduled for x-rays and they said they couldn't get me in. I couldn't believe that what I thought was going to be a routine x-ray was going to ruin the whole day. Dr. Man wanted to see my x-ray and I wouldn't have an up-to-date one. I wasn't happy at all. But Scott talked to the receptionists, and they managed to work me in after all. I have to thank Scott for that.

We got back to the main clinic and checked in at the always busy front desk. I was hoping my appointment would be on schedule, so we wouldn't miss our flight home. Today is my lucky day. Dr. Man is on schedule. He asked me the same questions he has always asked me at these follow up appointments. How am I feeling? How's the back feeling? And I would give him the same response as I did before. "My back is feeling good. I'm feeling good, no problems."

I was out of the exam room in fifteen or twenty minutes and we were on our way to getting on our flight back home. I decided at this time that if it was possible I could stop coming back for more check-ups. I figured if I had any complications, I'd have had them by now. I am going to call Dr. Man before my next appointment, tell him that I am fine and that I don't need another checkup. I think he'll understand.

March, 2006. I just returned from my fourth out of state trip to see Dr. Man for a follow-up appointment since my surgery a year ago. I was thinking about the first time I came to the Cleveland Clinic hoping Dr. Man would take my case and be able to fix the problems I was having with my spine. I remember looking out the cab window on my way to the clinic seeing everybody going about their normal Monday morning routines. But I was going to see this spinal surgeon about a very dangerous procedure so I could have a chance at as normal a quality of life as possible for me. A lot has happened in two years.

I am back in my routine of check-ups with Dr. Lowe every month. Everything is going fine as far as my health goes. The appointment consists of a blood draw and then Dr. Lowe comes in and he pulls my lab results up on the computer and points out areas of improvement and any areas of concern. He wants to find out if I have any changes, concerns, or questions for him. We discuss my chemo drugs and whether they are having a positive effect and whether we will continue down the same path of treatment. I usually don't. I say everything is fine. After he does his physical exam I start cracking a joke about anything that comes to mind because I can and it breaks up the tension of the appointment. I don't think he minds and he is usually laughing by the end of our discussions.

Once a month I receive my bone strengthening infusion called Zomata. It doesn't leave me with any side effects and I am thankful for that. I am on a pretty strict regime of eating right, exercising and getting as much sleep as I can. I don't take naps usually unless I'm beat and that hasn't happened for a long time.

When I first started going in for checkups, I had a number of x-rays taken, which are part of a skeletal survey to see how my bones are doing with the infusions and everything else I'm taking for the myeloma. Dr. Lowe found a spot on the upper inside of my right femur bone that's the size of a half penny and we're keeping an eye on it. The spot has been there for the longest time. It never changes shape but it's always there. I'm concerned but not worried, because being worried won't change anything. I'm not experiencing any pain but I know it's there.

Months later I have another routine x-ray on the same area. Dr. Lowe casually says the spot is not there anymore! WWWWhat? The drugs must be working. Why argue with good news? Just like that, a routine check-up can go in one's favor. I savor it because it doesn't happen often.

I ran into an old college buddy's brother in a locker room of all places. We were walking toward one another down the hall, and as our paths crossed I caught a glimpse of his face and said to myself, "I know that guy" but I kept on walking. I walked around the corner and sat down, wondering why he was there, since he didn't live anywhere nearby. A moment later, he came walking around the corner and introduced himself and we both said we thought we recognized one another. With a straight face, he said, "we all thought you were dead." It caught me off guard for a moment, and then I let out a short laugh. "No, I'm definitely still here, but I have a lot of stories because of it."

Chapter Thirty Seven

It Wasn't a Coincidence

I feel lucky having Dr. Lowe as my primary oncology doctor. Maybe it wasn't luck, maybe it was meant to be. He is close to my age and is easy to talk to. He does a great job of explaining things in lay terms. Dr. Lowe is always good at dealing with the "here and now" approach. He is ALWAYS up-front with me and my family. He's never seen the value in talking about what he would recommend in the future. In my case, you couldn't look too far down the road. We knew how serious it was.

When I was first admitted in the hospital he had to identify and prioritize all my health issues and determine what procedures or treatments he would use to fix them. He compartmentalized each problem and it simplified things for me. Otherwise, it would have really been overwhelming. I don't know how many doctors have had a patient come in with cancer, anemia, kidney failure, recurring pneumonia, fevers, excruciating back pain, skeletal issues, and successfully treat all those problems.

Finally, he had to deal with my post-surgery complications. He went against colleagues who advised him to give the case to someone else because the oncology department had never seen a situation like mine before. I never asked him afterwards if he ever considered deferring my case to someone he thought was more qualified. It doesn't really matter to me now anyway.

The other patients I've heard talking in the waiting area for check-ups always speak highly of having Dr. Lowe as their oncology doctor. All of my family is happy with the care he has given me over the years.

Having five sisters and a mother asking questions on my behalf, he's never wavered in responding to their concerns and listening to their ideas based on their research. I think he appreciates that they take the initiative to learn about myeloma and have gone to conferences in other parts of the country, such as the Twin cities and Little Rock, Arkansas, which is the headquarters of the myeloma research center.

By now I think he has a sense of their personalities and how to communicate best with each one or the whole family, when they all file in to meet with him during a family meeting. He knows the whole family's focus comes from their love for me.

He has been open minded enough to think outside the box to attain positive results for me. He has earned his pay on my case. Oh yeah, he has earned his pay. I don't think it's too far a stretch to say he will not see a case like mine again for awhile - maybe never.

Chapter Thirty Eight

My Angels

There have been numerous people over these past four years that have watched my back, did whatever it took to care for me, and always looked out for my interests. I wouldn't be where I am today without their compassion, integrity, love, support, and persistence. They have all displayed characteristics of great caregivers and are my angels that are continually watching over me. I never saw my parents get overwrought with emotion while I was going through all this but my sister told me that they would go out in the hall of the hospital or go into another room at home to vent their emotions. My parents are the strong trunk of the family tree and the rest of my family are all the branches that have sprouted and carried on their values and beliefs.

My Dad surprised me with how well he just rolled with whatever was happening. He was the best home health nurse I could have had. He never made a mistake in inserting the needles into my veins at home when giving me my infusions or shots in my belly. Dad knew how much I valued exercise and staying in shape. He walked with me all the time, down the hospital halls when I was hooked up to an IV line and oxygen. He walked with me when I had my back surgery and needed the walker to brace myself. He was right there all the time.

Dad drove me all over the place for my appointments and picked up my prescriptions. I really didn't miss driving, even though it drove me crazy when Dad got angry at the traffic and the traffic lights. I didn't drive my car for four years after I was diagnosed because it was too dangerous with my back problem and overall weakness. I really didn't miss it as much as I thought I would; my mind was elsewhere.

Dad would always help me put on my back brace (shell) and get me going to all my appointments. He did all this, never complained or made me feel like it was an imposition on his time. I think the best way you can repay somebody for their support and compassion is acknowledging them when it's much deserved, but not expected.

You know, I never saw my Dad get emotional about anything I was going through. It was just not his way. Considering all he went through in his life I'm not surprised. He was always there giving his time to help in my recovery. He is a tough, a very tough, stubborn Irish-Bohemian, who has the biggest heart when it comes to his family. Great job Dad, great job!!

Mum was my caregiver, nurse, dietician, advocate and psychologist. There isn't anyone else I would have wanted to be my primary caregiver. When she found out I had multiple myeloma she indicated that her sister had also had it and she began to become more educated on what it was and what types of treatments were available. She traveled with my sisters to Arkansas, Minneapolis, Chicago, Milwaukee, and Madison to attend educational sessions given by doctors, researchers, pharmaceutical companies, and dieticians. She attended the Myeloma Support Group meetings to gain additional information from actual patients and their families on care giving and daily issues. If I hadn't listened to her and gone into the hospital on more than one occasion when I had an infection, it could have been fatal according to Dr. Lowe.

Mum contacted the dietician at the hospital and they discussed what I should include in my diet when I am on chemotherapy. There were times that food I usually liked tasted terrible and that was due to my medications. The dietician provided Mum with a lot of information on what foods would help to keep weight on, foods that would still taste good, and foods that would not upset my stomach. She is not just a cook; my Mum is a chef. Her spaghetti is the best there is. Her enchiladas are also really good! I didn't think I'd like them but I do.

After I lost my appetite and taste buds due to the medications, she prepared dishes I needed to eat, not the food I wanted. She started to fix beets more often for meals. Beets provide a lot of iron and she felt I should be eating a lot of them to increase my red blood cells. I still hate beets! Mum attended seminars on how to cook for cancer patients and bought cookbooks that gave her guidance on foods to fix for me.

Mum was my nurse and kept track of when I should take my medications and when the prescriptions needed to be filled. She could tell when I was on too much medication that changed my moods. She would contact Dr. Lowe to determine which medication was affecting my mood and either reduce the dosage or find an alternative.

She would drive me to many of my appointments, spending countless hours and dollars on gas. Mum always made sure that I had clean bedding, clean clothes, and always reminded me to wash my hands, to make sure I wouldn't contract another infection. She would notify hospital staff if she felt that they were not following doctor's orders which could impact me in a negative way. An example would be in following the infectious disease doctor's orders on wearing masks, gowns, and gloves when in my hospital room. At times the hospital staff would pop in my room without the additional protection and she would notify the Nurse Manager. My Mum's faith gives her great comfort and strength. She went to mass every morning to pray for me as well as the rest of the family. I think all her prayers worked. She has always been there for me and she knows me better than anybody. She's the best…..she's the "Yoda of Mothers," Great job, Mum, Great job!

Both my Mum and Dad understood how important it was for me to have family around during the day when the rest of my family was at work. One or both of them would come and sit in my hospital room and quietly read. They knew there were times I just wanted quiet but also wanted someone there. I really appreciated their effort in sitting in my room during the day. There is no amount of words that I can say to thank my parents. They are the pillars of strength for our family.

Once I was admitted to the hospital, somebody had to take care of my bills and handle my finances. Sue, who is my financial power of attorney, took on the job. She had to identify what my expenses were, what financial resources I had, and where she could get assistance with covering the expenses. My medications were very expensive and she was very persistent in finding funding to cover them. She had to investigate my ability to receive disability payments and muddle through all the paperwork. When she looked through my checkbook she noticed the checks I had written to chiropractors, kinesiologists, and therapists for therapy on my back, which obviously didn't work. She contacted all of them and demanded they return all the money I paid them. The total amount was around two thousand dollars. She felt they had taken advantage of my situation just to make a buck. To my surprise every one of them paid back all the money I had paid them.

Sue called into the pharmaceutical company monthly to complete a phone survey before they would dispense my chemo drug. She worked with the pharmaceutical company to provide financial assistance to cover my very expensive medications. She dealt with the insurance company on paying my bills. I was definitely lucky to have her looking out for my welfare. Sue would setup, ask, and answer conference calls with doctors so family could get clarification on their concerns. I am thankful for all the journals she filled up with notes so I had something to reference when looking back and writing this book. I was glad that she was my advocate the night of my first back surgery and told those x-ray technicians to take a hike when they wanted to roll me onto a hard x-ray board. She would bring me newspapers and magazines every morning before work, when she could, when I was in the hospital. Let's not forget those mornings. Sue called Mum every morning to give her an update on how I was and what the plan was for the day. I know Mum and Dad were always waiting for that phone call. Thanks for everything Sue!

Peg was a great advocate for me. She was able to explain to family all the ins and outs of dealing with the medical profession. She enlightened everyone on the importance of communication among everyone in the family. Peg promoted the daily journal notes to minimize repetitive questions and use as a reference for the future. She went to my appointments, stayed with me when I was in the hospital, and attended doctor meetings. Peg always made time in her busy schedule to stop by before work or call to see if I needed anything or preferred to be left alone. Thanks for all the journals you filled with notes. I had no shortage of information to choose from. Peg is the fundraising and garage-sale queen, hands down! The money that was raised paid my medical bills, purchased my medications and contributed to my survival. Thanks for all your support, time and effort. You helped me out in so many ways. Thanks for everything Peg!

Jules was my traveling companion, who didn't take too long in saying yes if I needed something. She must have more e-mails on different doctors' consults than any caregiver. When my feet were swollen she bought me new shoes and purchased me a new winter coat when I needed one to fit over my back brace. The massages she gave helped to relax me and alleviate some of the pain I had. The travelling and investigating she did on finding solutions for my repetitive bouts with pneumonia and skeletal issues were invaluable. The walks she took with me outside helped me to escape from the hospital and enjoy the outdoors. Thanks for all the journals you filled with notes so I could write this book. I couldn't have done this without your help. Thanks for everything Jules!

Scott had his own business and somehow was able to make time for me while maintaining the business. He stayed with me at the hospital, getting anything I needed, walking with me in the halls, and talking about what was going on with the outside world. He gave me time to think about something else other than medical things. It is good to stay informed on what is going on with the rest of the world. He made the time to take me to my follow up appointment in Cleveland. The fundraiser at the brewery, where he helped set up all the sponsors and prizes, turned out great. I was able to pay for my medications, medical bills, and my survival with those funds. Thanks for everything Scott!